In order to succeed, your desire for success should be greater than your fear of failure.
Bill Cosby

Take up one idea. Make that one idea your life - think of it, dream of it, live on that idea. Let the brain, muscles, nerves, every part of your body, be full of that idea, and just leave every other idea alone. This is the way to success.
Swami Vivekananda

Always be yourself, express yourself, have faith in yourself, do not go out and look for a successful personality and duplicate it.
Bruce Lee

A successful man is one who can lay a firm foundation with the bricks others have thrown at him.
David Brinkley

Success is not final, failure is not fatal: it is the courage to continue that counts.
Winston Churchill

Think twice before you speak, because your words and influence will plant the seed of either success or failure in the mind of another.
Napoleon Hill

Success consists of going from failure to failure without loss of enthusiasm.

Winston Churchill

Try not to become a man of success, but rather try to become a man of value.
Albert Einstein

I don't know the key to success, but the key to failure is trying to please everybody.
Bill Cosby

Always bear in mind that your own resolution to succeed is more important than any other.
Abraham Lincoln

I've failed over and over and over again in my life and that is why I succeed.
Michael Jordan

Coming together is a beginning keeping together is progress working together is success.
Henry Ford

Don't aim for success if you want it just do what you love and believe in, and it will come naturally.
David Frost

The difference between a successful person and others is not a lack of strength, not a lack of knowledge, but rather a lack of will.
Vince Lombardi

Success is to be measured not so much by the position that one has reached in life as by the obstacles which he has overcome.
Booker T. Washington

No man succeeds without a good woman behind him. Wife or mother, if it is both, he is twice blessed indeed.
Godfrey Winn

Formula for success: rise early, work hard, strike oil.
J. Paul Getty

Formal education will make you a living self-education will make you a fortune.
Jim Rohn

If at first you don't succeed, try, try again. Then quit. There's no point in being a damn fool about it.
W. C. Fields

Develop success from failures. Discouragement and failure are two of the surest stepping stones to success.
Dale Carnegie

All you need is ignorance and confidence and the success is sure.
Mark Twain

Success is a lousy teacher. It seduces smart people into thinking they can't lose.
Bill Gates

I honestly think it is better to be a failure at something you love than to be a success at something you hate.
George Burns

Action is the foundational key to all success.
Pablo Picasso

To succeed in life, you need two things: ignorance and confidence.
Mark Twain

Failure is success if we learn from it.
Malcolm Forbes

What is success? I think it is a mixture of having a flair for the thing that you are doing knowing that it is not enough, that you have got to have hard work and a certain sense of purpose.
Margaret Thatcher

I don't measure a man's success by how high he climbs but how high he bounces when he hits bottom.

George S. Patton

To know even one life has breathed easier because you have lived. This is to have succeeded.
Ralph Waldo Emerson

It is no use saying, 'We are doing our best.' You have got to succeed in doing what is necessary.
Winston Churchill

Defeat is not the worst of failures. Not to have tried is the true failure.   **George Edward Woodberry**

Success or failure depends more upon attitude than upon capacity successful men act as though they have accomplished or are enjoying something. Soon it becomes a reality. Act, look, feel successful, conduct yourself accordingly, and you will be amazed at the positive results.
William James

A person with a new idea is a crank until the idea succeeds.
Mark Twain

Success depends upon previous preparation, and without such preparation there is sure to be failure.
Confucius

Success is not measured by what you accomplish, but by the opposition you have encountered, and the courage with which you have maintained the struggle against overwhelming odds.

Orison Swett Marden

Frustration, although quite painful at times, is a very positive and essential part of success.
Bo Bennett

Success is a science if you have the conditions, you get the result.
Oscar Wilde

The most important single ingredient in the formula of success is knowing how to get along with people.
Theodore Roosevelt

What's money? A man is a success if he gets up in the morning and goes to bed at night and in between does what he wants to do.
Bob Dylan

As kids we're not taught how to deal with success we're taught how to deal with failure. If at first you don't succeed, try, try again. If at first you succeed, then what?
Charlie Sheen

Winning isn't everything, it's the only thing.
Vince Lombardi

Belief in oneself is one of the most important bricks in building any successful venture.
Lydia M. Child

If everyone is moving forward together, then success takes care of itself.
Henry Ford

If you have no critics you'll likely have no success.
Malcolm X

One secret of success in life is for a man to be ready for his opportunity when it comes.
Benjamin Disraeli

Don't confuse fame with success. Madonna is one Helen Keller is the other.
Erma Bombeck

I have learned that success is to be measured not so much by the position that one has reached in life as by the obstacles which he has had to overcome while trying to succeed.
Booker T. Washington

Once you agree upon the price you and your family must pay for success, it enables you to ignore the minor hurts, the opponent's pressure, and the temporary failures.
Vince Lombardi

The ladder of success is best climbed by stepping on the rungs of opportunity.
Ayn Rand

Man needs his difficulties because they are necessary to enjoy success.
Abdul Kalam

Success is simple. Do what's right, the right way, at the right time.
Arnold H. Glasow

The successful man will profit from his mistakes and try again in a different way.
Dale Carnegie

Flaming enthusiasm, backed up by horse sense and persistence, is the quality that most frequently makes for success.
Dale Carnegie

Pray that success will not come any faster than you are able to endure it.
Elbert Hubbard

Failure is the key to success each mistake teaches us something.
Morihei Ueshiba

Happiness lies in the joy of achievement and the thrill of creative effort.
Franklin D. Roosevelt

Eighty percent of success is showing up.

Woody Allen

In order to succeed you must fail, so that you know what not to do the next time.
Anthony J. D'Angelo

Success is how high you bounce when you hit bottom.

George S. Patton

The starting point of all achievement is desire.
Napoleon Hill

In this world it is not what we take up, but what we give up, that makes us rich.
Henry Ward Beecher

There is only one success - to be able to spend your life in your own way.
Christopher Morley

Success isn't a result of spontaneous combustion. You must set yourself on fire.
Arnold H. Glasow

Most people give up just when they're about to achieve success. They quit on the one yard line. They give up at the last minute of the game one foot from a winning touchdown.
Ross Perot

Diligence is the mother of good fortune.
Benjamin Disraeli

I couldn't wait for success, so I went ahead without it.

Jonathan Winters

If you want to achieve things in life, you've just got to do them, and if you're talented and smart, you'll succeed.
Juliana Hatfield

Our worldly successes cannot be guaranteed, but our ability to achieve spiritual success is entirely up to us, thanks to the grace of God. The best advice I know is to give is to give those worldly things your best but never your all - reserve the ultimate hope for the only one who can grant it.
Mitt Romney

The greatest sign of success for a teacher... is to be able to say, 'The children are now working as if I did not exist.'
Maria Montessori

The common idea that success spoils people by making them vain, egotistic and self-complacent is erroneous on the contrary it makes them, for the most part, humble, tolerant and kind.
W. Somerset Maugham

The thermometer of success is merely the jealousy of the malcontents.
Salvador Dali

Success is falling nine times and getting up ten.
Jon Bon Jovi

If you wish to succeed in life, make perseverance your bosom friend, experience your wise counselor, caution your elder brother, and hope your guardian genius.
Joseph Addison

Success is dependent on effort.
Sophocles

They succeed, because they think they can.
Virgil

Success seems to be largely a matter of hanging on after others have let go.
William Feather

The measure of success is not whether you have a tough problem to deal with, but whether it is the same problem you had last year.
John Foster Dulles

Success is blocked by concentrating on it and planning for it... Success is shy - it won't come out while you're watching.
Tennessee Williams

It's our nature: Human beings like success but they hate successful people.
Carrot Top

Success is the child of drudgery and perseverance. It cannot be coaxed or bribed pay the price and it is yours.
Orison Swett Marden

Definiteness of purpose is the starting point of all achievement.
W. Clement Stone

Success in almost any field depends more on energy and drive than it does on intelligence. This explains why we have so many stupid leaders.
Sloan Wilson

Failure is not an option. Everyone has to succeed.
Arnold Schwarzenegger

Success is the one unpardonable sin against our fellows.
Ambrose Bierce

Success is counted sweetest by those who never succeed.
Emily Dickinson

How can they say my life is not a success? Have I not for more than sixty years got enough to eat and escaped being eaten?
Logan P. Smith

After I won the Oscar, my salary doubled, my friends tripled, my children became more popular at school, my butcher made a pass at me, and my maid hit me up for a raise.
Shirley Jones

Obedience is the mother of success and is wedded to safety.
Aeschylus

Success has a simple formula: do your best, and people may like it.
Sam Ewing

Success is not a good teacher, failure makes you humble.
Shahrukh Khan

Sometimes I worry about being a success in a mediocre world.
Lily Tomlin

Success is that old ABC - ability, breaks, and courage.

Charles Luckman

Success is like death. The more successful you become, the higher the houses in the hills get and the higher the fences get.
Kevin Spacey

Those who have succeeded at anything and don't mention luck are kidding themselves.
Larry King

Success is the progressive realization of predetermined, worthwhile, personal goals.
Paul J. Meyer

The man who has done his level best... is a success, even though the world may write him down a failure.
B. C. Forbes

Nothing succeeds like success.
Alexandre Dumas

We fall forward to succeed.
Mary Kay Ash

Success is simply a matter of luck. Ask any failure.
Earl Wilson

The toughest thing about success is that you've got to keep on being a success.
Irving Berlin

Nothing recedes like success.

Walter Winchell

Success is often the result of taking a misstep in the right direction.
Al Bernstein

The five essential entrepreneurial skills for success: Concentration, Discrimination, Organization, Innovation and Communication.
Harold S. Geneen

Success to me is having ten honeydew melons and eating only the top half of each slice.
Barbra Streisand

Success doesn't mean that you are healthy, success doesn't mean that you're happy, success doesn't mean that you're rested. Success really doesn't mean that you look good, or feel good, or are good.
Victoria Principal

It's not enough that I should succeed - others should fail.   David Merrick
Success is the space one occupies in the newspaper. Success is one day's insolence.
Elias Canetti

The one phrase you can use is that success has a thousand fathers, and failure is an orphan.
Alan Price

Your success and happiness lies in you. Resolve to keep happy, and your joy and you shall form an invincible host against difficulties.
Helen Keller

My mother was the most beautiful woman I ever saw. All I am I owe to my mother. I attribute all my success in life to the moral, intellectual and physical education I received from her.
George Washington

Character cannot be developed in ease and quiet. Only through experience of trial and suffering can the soul be strengthened, ambition inspired, and success achieved.
Helen Keller

We should measure welfare's success by how many people leave welfare, not by how many are added.
Ronald Reagan

Let every nation know, whether it wishes us well or ill, that we shall pay any price, bear any burden, meet any hardship, support any friend, oppose any foe to assure the survival and the success of liberty.
John F. Kennedy

The foundation stones for a balanced success are honesty, character, integrity, faith, love and loyalty.
Zig Ziglar

Put your heart, mind, and soul into even your smallest acts. This is the secret of success.
Swami Sivananda

The price of success is hard work, dedication to the job at hand, and the determination that whether we win or lose, we have applied the best of ourselves to the task at hand.
Vince Lombardi

There are no secrets to success. It is the result of preparation, hard work, and learning from failure.
Colin Powell

That some achieve great success, is proof to all that others can achieve it as well.
Abraham Lincoln

Israel was not created in order to disappear - Israel will endure and flourish. It is the child of hope and the home of the brave. It can neither be broken by adversity nor demoralized by success. It carries the shield of democracy and it honors the sword of freedom.
John F. Kennedy

The size of your success is measured by the strength of your desire the size of your dream and how you handle disappointment along the way.
Robert Kiyosaki

The only place success comes before work is in the dictionary.
Vince Lombardi

Patience, persistence and perspiration make an unbeatable combination for success.
Napoleon Hill

The secret of success is learning how to use pain and pleasure instead of having pain and pleasure use you. If you do that, you're in control of your life. If you don't, life controls you.
Tony Robbins

If you want to succeed you should strike out on new paths, rather than travel the worn paths of accepted success.
John D. Rockefeller

I believe that being successful means having a balance of success stories across the many areas of your life. You can't truly be considered successful in your business life if your home life is in shambles.
Zig Ziglar

It has always seemed strange to me... the things we admire in men, kindness and generosity, openness, honesty, understanding and feeling, are the concomitants of failure in our system. And those traits we detest, sharpness, greed, acquisitiveness, meanness, egotism and self-interest, are the traits of

success. And while men admire the quality of the first they love the produce of the second.
John Steinbeck

A little more persistence, a little more effort, and what seemed hopeless failure may turn to glorious success.

Elbert Hubbard

Part of the secret of a success in life is to eat what you like and let the food fight it out inside.
Mark Twain

Before success comes in any man's life, he's sure to meet with much temporary defeat and, perhaps some failures. When defeat overtakes a man, the easiest and the most logical thing to do is to quit. That's exactly what the majority of men do.
Napoleon Hill

It's fine to celebrate success but it is more important to heed the lessons of failure.
Bill Gates

Like success, failure is many things to many people. With Positive Mental Attitude, failure is a learning experience, a rung on the ladder, a plateau at which to get your thoughts in order and prepare to try again.

W. Clement Stone

Dictionary is the only place that success comes before work. Hard work is the price we must pay for success. I think you can accomplish anything if you're willing to pay the price.
Vince Lombardi

Without continual growth and progress, such words as improvement, achievement, and success have no meaning.
Benjamin Franklin

The supreme quality for leadership is unquestionably integrity. Without it, no real success is possible, no matter whether it is on a section gang, a football field, in an army, or in an office.
Dwight D. Eisenhower

Success is peace of mind which is a direct result of self-satisfaction in knowing you did your best to become the best you are capable of becoming.
John Wooden

Any fact facing us is not as important as our attitude toward it, for that determines our success or failure. The way you think about a fact may defeat you before you ever do anything about it. You are overcome by the fact because you think you are.
Norman Vincent Peale

Many of life's failures are people who did not realize how close they were to success when they gave up.

Thomas A. Edison

Success comes from taking the initiative and following up... persisting... eloquently expressing the depth of your love. What simple action could you take today to produce a new momentum toward success in your life?
Tony Robbins

Success is like reaching an important birthday and finding you're exactly the same.
Audrey Hepburn

Money and success don't change people they merely amplify what is already there.
Will Smith

I have learned, that if one advances confidently in the direction of his dreams, and endeavors to live the life he has imagined, he will meet with a success unexpected in common hours.
Henry David Thoreau

Applause waits on success.
Benjamin Franklin

Never lose sight of the fact that the most important yardstick of your success will be how you treat other people - your family, friends, and coworkers, and even strangers you meet along the way.
Barbara Bush

The best revenge is massive success.
Frank Sinatra

The first step toward success is taken when you refuse to be a captive of the environment in which you first find yourself.
Mark Caine

The superior man makes the difficulty to be overcome his first interest success only comes later.
Confucius

Success does not consist in never making mistakes but in never making the same one a second time.
George Bernard Shaw

A true friend is one who overlooks your failures and tolerates your success!
Doug Larson

Success makes so many people hate you. I wish it wasn't that way. It would be wonderful to enjoy success without seeing envy in the eyes of those around you.
Marilyn Monroe

Money won't create success, the freedom to make it will.   Nelson Mandela
Success has always been a great liar.
Friedrich Nietzsche

My definition of success is to live your life in a way that causes you to feel a ton of pleasure and very little pain - and because of your lifestyle, have the people around you feel a lot more pleasure than they do pain.

Tony Robbins

Honesty and integrity are absolutely essential for success in life - all areas of life. The really good news is that anyone can develop both honesty and integrity.

Zig Ziglar

You cannot climb the ladder of success dressed in the costume of failure.
Zig Ziglar

Success is not the key to happiness. Happiness is the key to success. If you love what you are doing, you will be successful.
Albert Schweitzer

We must walk consciously only part way toward our goal, and then leap in the dark to our success.
Henry David Thoreau

Success is steady progress toward one's personal goals.
Jim Rohn

Success usually comes to those who are too busy to be looking for it.
Henry David Thoreau

Every day is a new opportunity. You can build on yesterday's success or put its failures behind and start over again. That's the way life is, with a new game every day, and that's the way baseball is.
Bob Feller

The way a team plays as a whole determines its success. You may have the greatest bunch of individual stars in the world, but if they don't play together, the club won't be worth a dime.
Babe Ruth

Success is the result of perfection, hard work, learning from failure, loyalty, and persistence.
Colin Powell

The secret to success is to offend the greatest number of people.
George Bernard Shaw

The only thing I'm addicted to is winning. This bootleg cult, arrogantly referred to as Alcoholics Anonymous, reports a 5 percent success rate. My success rate is 100 percent.
Charlie Sheen

Success is neither magical nor mysterious. Success is the natural consequence of consistently applying the basic fundamentals.
Jim Rohn

Success is nothing more than a few simple disciplines, practiced every day.
Jim Rohn

Successful people make money. It's not that people who make money become successful, but that successful people attract money. They bring success to what they do.
Wayne Dyer

Most great people have attained their greatest success just one step beyond their greatest failure.
Napoleon Hill

Discipline is the soul of an army. It makes small numbers formidable procures success to the weak, and esteem to all.
George Washington

Success is dependent upon the glands - sweat glands.

Zig Ziglar

If there is any one secret of success, it lies in the ability to get the other person's point of view and see

things from that person's angle as well as from your own.
Henry Ford

Four things for success: work and pray, think and believe.
Norman Vincent Peale

A graduation ceremony is an event where the commencement speaker tells thousands of students dressed in identical caps and gowns that 'individuality' is the key to success.
Robert Orben

Success is doing ordinary things extraordinarily well.
Jim Rohn

You do not pay the price of success, you enjoy the price of success.
Zig Ziglar

Every person who wins in any undertaking must be willing to cut all sources of retreat. Only by doing so can one be sure of maintaining that state of mind known as a burning desire to win - essential to success.
Napoleon Hill

You are a product of your environment. So choose the environment that will best develop you toward your objective. Analyze your life in terms of its

environment. Are the things around you helping you toward success - or are they holding you back?
W. Clement Stone

Success is not to be pursued it is to be attracted by the person you become.
Jim Rohn.

Never continue in a job you don't enjoy. If you're happy in what you're doing, you'll like yourself, you'll have inner peace. And if you have that, along with physical health, you will have had more success than you could possibly have imagined.
Johnny Carson

Success is the maximum utilization of the ability that you have.
Zig Ziglar

How many a man has thrown up his hands at a time when a little more effort, a little more patience would have achieved success.
Elbert Hubbard

That man is a success who has lived well, laughed often and loved much.
Robert Louis Stevenson

The most glorious moments in your life are not the so-called days of success, but rather those days when out of dejection and despair you feel rise in you a

challenge to life, and the promise of future accomplishments.
Gustave Flaubert

The test of success is not what you do when you are on top. Success is how high you bounce when you hit bottom.
George S. Patton

The line between failure and success is so fine that we scarcely know when we pass it: so fine that we are often on the line and do not know it.
Elbert Hubbard

Old age is like everything else. To make a success of it, you've got to start young.
Theodore Roosevelt

Before everything else, getting ready is the secret of success.
Henry Ford

Every success story has a parent who says, 'over my dead body.' Every success story has an old person who walks up to you and says, when you're acting the fool, 'you know I worry about you sometimes.'
Bill Cosby

He has achieved success who has worked well, laughed often, and loved much.
Elbert Hubbard

What material success does is provide you with the ability to concentrate on other things that really matter. And that is being able to make a difference, not only in your own life, but in other people's lives.
Oprah Winfrey

Microsoft has had two goals in the last 10 years. One was to copy the Mac, and the other was to copy Lotus' success in the spreadsheet - basically, the applications business. And over the course of the last 10 years, Microsoft accomplished both of those goals. And now they are completely lost.
Steve Jobs

We learned about honesty and integrity - that the truth matters... that you don't take shortcuts or play by your own set of rules... and success doesn't count unless you earn it fair and square.
Michelle Obama

For unflagging interest and enjoyment, a household of children, if things go reasonably well, certainly all other forms of success and achievement lose their importance by comparison.
Theodore Roosevelt

Our goals can only be reached through a vehicle of a plan, in which we must fervently believe, and upon which we must vigorously act. There is no other route to success.

Pablo Picasso

The path to success is to take massive, determined action.
Tony Robbins

America is the most grandiose experiment the world has seen, but, I am afraid, it is not going to be a success.
Sigmund Freud

Tell me, why is the media here so negative? Why are we in India so embarrassed to recognise our own strengths, our achievements? We are such a great nation. We have so many amazing success stories but we refuse to acknowledge them. Why?
Abdul Kalam

Success is often achieved by those who don't know that failure is inevitable.
Coco Chanel

My parents shared not only an improbable love, they shared an abiding faith in the possibilities of this nation. They would give me an African name, Barack, or blessed, believing that in a tolerant America your name is no barrier to success.
Barack Obama

Focused, hard work is the real key to success. Keep your eyes on the goal, and just keep taking the next step towards completing it. If you aren't sure which

way to do something, do it both ways and see which works better.
John Carmack

She's the kind of girl who climbed the ladder of success wrong by wrong.
Mae West
Success demands singleness of purpose.
Vince Lombardi

Whosoever desires constant success must change his conduct with the times.
Niccolo Machiavelli

There is nothing more difficult to take in hand, more perilous to conduct, or more uncertain in its success, than to take the lead in the introduction of a new order of things.
Niccolo Machiavelli

No man ever achieved worth-while success who did not, at one time or other, find himself with at least one foot hanging well over the brink of failure.
Napoleon Hill

Personality is the most important thing to an actress's success.
Mae West

Success is almost totally dependent upon drive and persistence. The extra energy required to make

another effort or try another approach is the secret of winning.
Denis Waitley

The key to success is to focus our conscious mind on things we desire not things we fear.
Brian Tracy

There is no force like success, and that is why the individual makes all effort to surround himself throughout life with the evidence of it as of the individual, so should it be of the nation.
Marcus Garvey

Success is getting what you want. Happiness is liking what you get.
H. Jackson Brown, Jr.

Success in its highest and noblest form calls for peace of mind and enjoyment and happiness which come only to the man who has found the work that he likes best.
Napoleon Hill

There's no abiding success without commitment.
Tony Robbins

Success is peace of mind, which is a direct result of self-satisfaction in knowing you made the effort to become the best of which you are capable.
John Wooden

If you wish to be a success in the world, promise everything, deliver nothing.
Napoleon Bonaparte

There is probably a perverse pride in my administration... that we were going to do the right thing, even if short-term it was unpopular. And I think anybody who's occupied this office has to remember that success is determined by an intersection in policy and politics and that you can't be neglecting of marketing and P.R. and public opinion.
Barack Obama

I do not think that there is any other quality so essential to success of any kind as the quality of perseverance. It overcomes almost everything, even nature.
John D. Rockefeller

One man cannot practice many arts with success.
Plato

You know you are on the road to success if you would do your job, and not be paid for it.
Oprah Winfrey

An artist cannot fail it is a success to be one.
Charles Horton Cooley

My success was not based so much on any great intelligence but on great common sense.
Helen Gurley Brown

I stand ready to lead us down a different path where we're lifted up by our desire to succeed, not dragged down by a resentment of success.
Mitt Romney

You grow up a bit damaged or broken then you have some success but you don't know how to feel good about the work you're doing or the life you're leading.

Johnny Depp

The ladder of success is never crowded at the top.
Napoleon Hill

If you have a success you have it for the wrong reasons. If you become popular it is always because of the worst aspects of your work.
Ernest Hemingway

Those who cannot work with their hearts achieve but a hollow, half-hearted success that breeds bitterness all around.
Abdul Kalam

Anything that won't sell, I don't want to invent. Its sale is proof of utility, and utility is success.
Thomas A. Edison

You might well remember that nothing can bring you success but yourself.
Napoleon Hill

A rejection is nothing more than a necessary step in the pursuit of success.
Bo Bennett

I do not think there is any thrill that can go through the human heart like that felt by the inventor as he sees some creation of the brain unfolding to success... such emotions make a man forget food, sleep, friends, love, everything.
Nikola Tesla

The battle of life is, in most cases, fought uphill and to win it without a struggle were perhaps to win it without honor. If there were no difficulties there would be no success if there were nothing to struggle for, there would be nothing to be achieved.
Samuel Smiles

The central conservative truth is that it is culture, not politics, that determines the success of a society. The central liberal truth is that politics can change a culture and save it from itself.
Daniel Patrick Moynihan

Management is efficiency in climbing the ladder of success leadership determines whether the ladder is leaning against the right wall.

Stephen Covey

Forward, as occasion offers. Never look round to see whether any shall note it... Be satisfied with success in even the smallest matter, and think that even such a result is no trifle.
Marcus Aurelius

We're constantly striving for success, fame and comfort when all we really need to be happy is someone or some thing to be enthusiastic about.
H. Jackson Brown, Jr.

You never achieve success unless you like what you are doing.
Dale Carnegie

Men of age object too much, consult too long, adventure too little, repent too soon, and seldom drive business home to the full period, but content themselves with a mediocrity of success.
Dale Carnegie

A constant struggle, a ceaseless battle to bring success from inhospitable surroundings, is the price of all great achievements.
Orison Swett Marden

Ask yourself the secret of your success. Listen to your answer, and practice it.
Richard Bach

The key to success is to keep growing in all areas of life - mental, emotional, spiritual, as well as physical.
Julius Erving

Obstacles are necessary for success because in selling, as in all careers of importance, victory comes only after many struggles and countless defeats.
Og Mandino

You do the work and you want people to see it but, um while I'm doing the work, the result doesn't matter at all to me. Ultimately, I don't, I don't care whether the film is - you know - some big giant box-office bonanza and I don't care if its a complete flop. To me, when a film gets made and it's actually finished it's a success. They're all a success in their own way.
Johnny Depp

If a man loves the labour of his trade, apart from any question of success or fame, the gods have called him.

Robert Louis Stevenson

There is little success where there is little laughter.
Andrew Carnegie

It is not the going out of port, but the coming in, that determines the success of a voyage.
Henry Ward Beecher

If we become one of those societies that attack success, why not come as certain there will be a lot less success? And that's not who we are.
Mitt Romney

That business we started with 10 people has now grown into a great American success story.
Mitt Romney

Success is not greedy, as people think, but insignificant. That is why it satisfies nobody.
Lucius Annaeus Seneca

I must admit that I personally measure success in terms of the contributions an individual makes to her or his fellow human beings.
Margaret Mead

The ability to convert ideas to things is the secret of outward success.
Henry Ward Beecher

In all our deeds, the proper value and respect for time determines success or failure.
Malcolm X

Achievement is not always success, while reputed failure often is. It is honest endeavor, persistent effort to do the best possible under any and all circumstances.
Orison Swett Marden

Success is dangerous. One begins to copy oneself, and to copy oneself is more dangerous than to copy others. It leads to sterility.
Pablo Picasso

Success is full of promise till one gets it, and then it seems like a nest from which the bird has flown.
Henry Ward Beecher

Perseverance is a great element of success. If you only knock long enough and loud enough at the gate, you are sure to wake up somebody.
Henry Wadsworth Longfellow

Everyone who achieves success in a great venture, solves each problem as they came to it. They helped themselves. And they were helped through powers known and unknown to them at the time they set out on their voyage. They keep going regardless of the obstacles they met.
W. Clement Stone

In inner-city, low-income communities of color, there's such a high correlation in terms of educational quality and success.
Bill Gates

I think you can have 10,000 explanations for failure, but no good explanation for success.
Paulo Coelho

Well I think any author or musician is anxious to have legitimate sales of their products, partly so they're rewarded for their success, partly so they can go on and do new things.
Bill Gates

One important key to success is self-confidence. An important key to self-confidence is preparation.
Arthur Ashe

Our success educationally, industrially and politically is based upon the protection of a nation founded by ourselves. And the nation can be nowhere else but in Africa.
Marcus Garvey

I owe my success to having listened respectfully to the very best advice, and then going away and doing the exact opposite.
Gilbert K. Chesterton

One might think that the money value of an invention constitutes its reward to the man who loves his work. But... I continue to find my greatest pleasure, and so my reward, in the work that precedes what the world calls success.
Thomas A. Edison

I find my greatest pleasure, and so my reward, in the work that precedes what the world calls success.

Thomas A. Edison

Success is achieved and maintained by those who try and keep trying.
W. Clement Stone

We learned about gratitude and humility - that so many people had a hand in our success, from the teachers who inspired us to the janitors who kept our school clean... and we were taught to value everyone's contribution and treat everyone with respect.
Michelle Obama

Procrastination is one of the most common and deadliest of diseases and its toll on success and happiness is heavy.
Wayne Gretzky

Perseverance - a lowly virtue whereby mediocrity achieves an inglorious success.
Ambrose Bierce

Success in life is founded upon attention to the small things rather than to the large things to the every day things nearest to us rather than to the things that are remote and uncommon.
Booker T. Washington

Our limitations and success will be based, most often, on your own expectations for ourselves. What the mind dwells upon, the body acts upon.
Denis Waitley

If a man has been his mother's undisputed darling he retains throughout life the triumphant feeling, the confidence in success, which not seldom brings actual success along with it.
Sigmund Freud

In the United States, I am a great success, but I am not a celebrity.
Paulo Coelho

A great social success is a pretty girl who plays her cards as carefully as if she were plain.
F. Scott Fitzgerald

I'm an addict, I'm addicted to success. Thankfully, there's no rehab for success.
Lil Wayne

Seventy percent of success in life is showing up.
Woody Allen

I attribute my success to this - I never gave or took any excuse.
Florence Nightingale

Through perseverance many people win success out of what seemed destined to be certain failure.
Benjamin Disraeli

At the end of the day, the most overwhelming key to a child's success is the positive involvement of parents.
Jane D. Hull

Success consecrates the most offensive crimes.
Lucius Annaeus Seneca

Communication - the human connection - is the key to personal and career success.
Paul J. Meyer

Sound character provides the power with which a person may ride the emergencies of life instead of being overwhelmed by them. Failure is... the highway to success.
Og Mandino

To many a man, and sometimes to a youth, there comes the opportunity to choose between honorable competence and tainted wealth. The young man who starts out to be poor and honorable, holds in his hand one of the strongest elements of success.
Orison Swett Marden

Success is having to worry about every damn thing in the world, except money.

Johnny Cash

Have regular hours for work and play make each day
both useful and pleasant, and prove that you
understand the worth of time by employing it well.
Then youth will be delightful, old age will bring few
regrets, and life will become a beautiful success.
Louisa May Alcott

Forget about the consequences of failure. Failure is
only a temporary change in direction to set you
straight for your next success.
Denis Waitley

Personal satisfaction is the most important ingredient
of success.
Denis Waitley

The winner's edge is not in a gifted birth, a high IQ, or
in talent. The winner's edge is all in the attitude, not
aptitude. Attitude is the criterion for success.
Denis Waitley

A strong, positive self-image is the best possible
preparation for success.
Joyce Brothers

Time is the most precious element of human
existence. The successful person knows how to put
energy into time and how to draw success from time.
Denis Waitley

The greatest thing a man can do in this world is to make the most possible out of the stuff that has been given him. This is success, and there is no other.
Orison Swett Marden

Success is a great deodorant.
Elizabeth Taylor

The secret of success is constancy to purpose.
Benjamin Disraeli

Learning and innovation go hand in hand. The arrogance of success is to think that what you did yesterday will be sufficient for tomorrow.
William Pollard

The great secret of success is to go through life as a man who never gets used up.
Albert Schweitzer

Almost no one is foolish enough to imagine that he automatically deserves great success in any field of activity yet almost everyone believes that he automatically deserves success in marriage.
Sidney J. Harris

No one has a corner on success. It is his who pays the price.
Orison Swett Marden

The secret of success is to be ready when your opportunity comes.
Benjamin Disraeli

A great secret of success is to go through life as a man who never gets used up.
Albert Schweitzer

If I die prematurely I shall be saved from being bored to death at my own success.
Samuel Butler

Success without honor is an unseasoned dish it will satisfy your hunger, but it won't taste good.
Joe Paterno

All that is necessary to break the spell of inertia and frustration is this: Act as if it were impossible to fail. That is the talisman, the formula, the command of right about face which turns us from failure to success.
Dorthea Brande

Success is the child of audacity.
Benjamin Disraeli

Success didn't spoil me, I've always been insufferable.

Fran Lebowitz

Success isn't measured by money or power or social rank. Success is measured by your discipline and inner peace.
Mike Ditka

Not every difficult and dangerous thing is suitable for training, but only that which is conducive to success in achieving the object of our effort.
Epictetus

Youth is not enough. And love is not enough. And success is not enough. And, if we could achieve it, enough would not be enough.
Mignon McLaughlin

I just go where my heart tells me, where my gut tells me to go, where I'm enjoying my life the most, where I feel like I can have the most success. I've truly enjoyed my experience in NASCAR, to the point that I want to do it full time.
Danica Patrick

Every failure is a step to success.
William Whewell

The more tranquil a man becomes, the greater is his success, his influence, his power for good. Calmness of mind is one of the beautiful jewels of wisdom.
James Allen

Success in life comes not from holding a good hand, but in playing a poor hand well.
Denis Waitley

I'd rather be a failure at something I love than a success at something I hate.
George Burns

No man can be a failure if he thinks he's a success If he thinks he is a winner, then he is.
Robert W. Service

You will be a failure, until you impress the subconscious with the conviction you are a success. This is done by making an affirmation which 'clicks.'
Florence Scovel Shinn

I remember one day sitting at the pool and suddenly the tears were streaming down my cheeks. Why was I so unhappy? I had success. I had security. But it wasn't enough. I was exploding inside.
Ingrid Bergman

The secret of success in life is for a man to be ready for his opportunity when it comes.
Benjamin Disraeli

King Louis Philippe once said to me that he attributed the great success of the British nation in political life to their talking politics after dinner.
Benjamin Disraeli

If we get our self-esteem from superficial places, from our popularity, appearance, business success, financial situation, health, any of these, we will be disappointed, because no one can guarantee that we'll have them tomorrow.
Kathy Ireland

Failure is not our only punishment for laziness there is also the success of others.
Jules Renard

Life affords no higher pleasure than that of surmounting difficulties, passing from one step of success to another, forming new wishes and seeing them gratified.
Samuel Johnson

The best augury of a man's success in his profession is that he thinks it the finest in the world.
George Eliot

Success is not built on success. It's built on failure. It's built on frustration. Sometimes its built on catastrophe.
Sumner Redstone

Each success only buys an admission ticket to a more difficult problem.
Henry A. Kissinger

The success I have achieved in bodybuilding, motion pictures, and business would not have been possible without the generosity of the American people and the freedom here to pursue your dreams.
Arnold Schwarzenegger

If I had permitted my failures, or what seemed to me at the time a lack of success, to discourage me I cannot see any way in which I would ever have made progress.
Calvin Coolidge

Success can make you go one of two ways. It can make you a prima donna - or it can smooth the edges, take away the insecurities, let the nice things come out.
Barbara Walters

Success comes when people act together failure tends to happen alone.
Deepak Chopra

I have no problem with the people who work hard to get success. But I think people are very jealous about success. I work very hard and they don't appreciate that.
Alain Prost

Humor has bailed me out of more tight situations than I can think of. If you go with your instincts and keep

your humor, creativity follows. With luck, success comes, too.
Jimmy Buffett

The idea of capitalism is not just success but also the failure that allows success to happen.
P. J. O'Rourke

Everything I have, my career, my success, my family, I owe to America.
Arnold Schwarzenegger

Creative risk taking is essential to success in any goal where the stakes are high. Thoughtless risks are destructive, of course, but perhaps even more wasteful is thoughtless caution which prompts inaction and promotes failure to seize opportunity.
Gary Ryan Blair

In order that people may be happy in their work, these three things are needed: They must be fit for it. They must not do too much of it. And they must have a sense of success in it.
John Ruskin

An excuse becomes an obstacle in your journey to success when it is made in place of your best effort or when it is used as the object of the blame.
Bo Bennett

They talk about the failure of socialism but where is the success of capitalism in Africa, Asia and Latin America?
Fidel Castro

The talent of success is nothing more than doing what you can do well, and doing well whatever you do without thought of fame. If it comes at all it will come because it is deserved, not because it is sought after.
Henry Wadsworth Longfellow

The envious man grows lean at the success of his neighbor.
Horace

No one who achieves success does so without acknowledging the help of others. The wise and confident acknowledge this help with gratitude.
Alfred North Whitehead

Within the hearts men, loyalty and consideration are esteemed greater than success.
Bryant H. McGill

What I have in common with the character in 'Truman' is this incredible need to please people. I feel like I want to take care of everyone and I also feel this terrible guilt if I am unable to. And I have felt this way ever since all this success started.
Jim Carrey

We can come to look upon the deaths of our enemies with as much regret as we feel for those of our friends, namely, when we miss their existence as witnesses to our success.
Arthur Schopenhauer

No foreign policy - no matter how ingenious - has any chance of success if it is born in the minds of a few and carried in the hearts of none.
Henry A. Kissinger

The secret to success is good leadership, and good leadership is all about making the lives of your team members or workers better.
Tony Dungy

The Lord gave us two ends - one to sit on and the other to think with. Success depends on which one we use the most.
Ann Landers

Whether you come from a council estate or a country estate, your success will be determined by your own confidence and fortitude.
Michelle Obama

The season of failure is the best time for sowing the seeds of success.
Paramahansa Yogananda

It is only the cynicism that is born of success that is penetrating and valid.
George Jean Nathan

Always remember that striving and struggle precede success, even in the dictionary.
Sarah Ban Breathnach

No one succeeds without effort... Those who succeed owe their success to perseverance.
Ramana Maharshi

The road to success is always under construction.
Lily Tomlin

Raising children is an uncertain thing success is reached only after a life of battle and worry.
Democritus

If you work just for money, you'll never make it, but if you love what you're doing and you always put the customer first, success will be yours.
Ray Kroc

Along with success comes a reputation for wisdom.
Euripides

It's very easy for me to say what success is. I think success is connecting with an audience who understands you and having a dialogue with them. I think success is continuing to push yourself forward

creatively and not sort of becoming a caricature of yourself.
Lena Dunham

I can honestly say that I was never affected by the question of the success of an undertaking. If I felt it was the right thing to do, I was for it regardless of the possible outcome.
Golda Meir

When you see something that is technically sweet, you go ahead and do it and you argue about what to do about it only after you have had your technical success. That is the way it was with the atomic bomb.

J. Robert Oppenheimer

Hope is a state of mind, not of the world. Hope, in this deep and powerful sense, is not the same as joy that things are going well, or willingness to invest in enterprises that are obviously heading for success, but rather an ability to work for something because it is good.
Vaclav Havel

Honesty is the cornerstone of all success, without which confidence and ability to perform shall cease to exist.
Mary Kay Ash

Success or failure in business is caused more by the mental attitude even than by mental capacities.
Walter Scott

Success is the progressive realization of a worthy goal or ideal.
Earl Nightingale

There's no secret about success. Did you ever know a successful man who didn't tell you about it?
Kin Hubbard

There is no success without hardship.
Sophocles

Willpower is the key to success. Successful people strive no matter what they feel by applying their will to overcome apathy, doubt or fear.
Dan Millman

I'm not after fame and success and fortune and power. It's mostly that I want to have a good job and have good friends that's the good stuff in life.
Drew Barrymore

Success follows doing what you want to do. There is no other way to be successful.
Malcolm Forbes

It is wise to keep in mind that neither success nor failure is ever final.

Roger Babson

After my spectacular failures, I could not be satisfied with an ordinary success.
Mason Cooley

A desire to be in charge of our own lives, a need for control, is born in each of us. It is essential to our mental health, and our success, that we take control.
Robert Foster Bennett

I've been so fortunate in my life that my family has never been jealous of my success. They have shown true love and commitment to me by being supportive. They shared in it.
Mike Krzyzewski

In Hollywood a marriage is a success if it outlasts milk.
Rita Rudner

Whenever an individual or a business decides that success has been attained, progress stops.
Thomas J. Watson

I am doomed to an eternity of compulsive work. No set goal achieved satisfies. Success only breeds a new goal. The golden apple devoured has seeds. It is endless.
Bette Davis

Mohammed was not an apparent failure. He was a dazzling success, politically as well as spiritually, and Islam went from strength to strength to strength.
Karen Armstrong

No experience is a cause of success or failure. We do not suffer from the shock of our experiences, so-called trauma - but we make out of them just what suits our purposes.
Alfred Adler

The freedom to fail is vital if you're going to succeed. Most successful people fail from time to time, and it is a measure of their strength that failure merely propels them into some new attempt at success.
Michael Korda

Success in any endeavor depends on the degree to which it is an expression of your true self.
Ralph Marston

To have long term success as a coach or in any position of leadership, you have to be obsessed in some way.
Pat Riley

Be yourself. Follow your instincts. Success depends, at least in part, on the ability to 'carry it off.'
Donald Rumsfeld

Failure is only postponed success as long as courage 'coaches' ambition. The habit of persistence is the habit of victory.
Herbert Kaufman

The compensation of a very early success is a conviction that life is a romantic matter. In the best sense one stays young.
F. Scott Fitzgerald

However things may seem, no evil thing is success and no good thing is failure.
Henry Wadsworth Longfellow

I've learned that mistakes can often be as good a teacher as success.
Jack Welch

Success is not in what you have, but who you are.
Bo Bennett

Education is the key to success in life, and teachers make a lasting impact in the lives of their students.
Solomon Ortiz

Desire is the key to motivation, but it's the determination and commitment to unrelenting pursuit of your goal - a commitment to excellence - that will enable you to attain the success you seek.
Mario Andretti

I did stand-up comedy for 18 years. Ten of those years were spent learning, four years were spent refining, and four years were spent in wild success. I was seeking comic originality, and fame fell on me as a byproduct. The course was more plodding than heroic.
Steve Martin

We learn wisdom from failure much more than from success. We often discover what will do, by finding out what will not do and probably he who never made a mistake never made a discovery.
Samuel Smiles

When it comes to success, there are no shortcuts.
Bo Bennett

The decadent international but individualistic capitalism in the hands of which we found ourselves after the war is not a success. It is not intelligent. It is not beautiful. It is not just. It is not virtuous. And it doesn't deliver the goods.
John Maynard Keynes

For true success ask yourself these four questions: Why? Why not? Why not me? Why not now?
James Allen

No student ever attains very eminent success by simply doing what is required of him: it is the amount

and excellence of what is over and above the required, that determines the greatness of ultimate distinction.
Charles Kendall Adams

When I prayed for success, I forgot to ask for sound sleep and good digestion.
Mason Cooley

The world judge of men by their ability in their profession, and we judge of ourselves by the same test: for it is on that on which our success in life depends.
William Hazlitt

Success seems to be connected with action. Successful people keep moving. They make mistakes, but they don't quit.
Conrad Hilton

Success is a beast. And it actually puts the emphasis on the wrong thing. You get away with more instead of looking within.
Brad Pitt

While I was doing stand-up, I thought I knew for sure that success meant getting everyone to like me. So I became whoever I thought people wanted me to be. I'd say yes when I wanted to say no, and I even wore a few dresses.
Ellen DeGeneres

Whether a party can have much success without a woman present I must ask others to decide, but one thing is certain, no party is any fun unless seasoned with folly.
Desiderius Erasmus

Keep in mind that neither success nor failure is ever final.
Roger Babson

When I finish a picture I don't show it to anyone if I feel it's not good enough yet. I've learnt to listen to my partners and my friends. For me it's the biggest success if they like it.
Marilyn Manson

The secret of my success is a two word answer: Know people.
Harvey S. Firestone

I'm hopeful. I know there is a lot of ambition in Washington, obviously. But I hope the ambitious realize that they are more likely to succeed with success as opposed to failure.
George W. Bush

The concept of the 'good ol' days' must be one of our society's biggest delusions, top reasons for depression, as well as most often used excuse for lack of success.
Bo Bennett

A government for the people must depend for its success on the intelligence, the morality, the justice, and the interest of the people themselves.
Grover Cleveland

Enjoy your sweat because hard work doesn't guarantee success, but without it you don't have a chance.
Alex Rodriguez

Never mind what others do do better than yourself, beat your own record from day to day, and you are a success.
William J. H. Boetcker

Success is where preparation and opportunity meet.
Bobby Unser

For success, attitude is equally as important as ability.

Walter Scott

If success is a habit, it is a hard one to acquire.
Mason Cooley

Enjoying success requires the ability to adapt. Only by being open to change will you have a true opportunity to get the most from your talent.
Nolan Ryan

We must believe in luck. For how else can we explain the success of those we don't like?
Jean Cocteau

The more defects a man may have, the older he is, the less lovable, the more resounding his success.
Marquis de Sade

The only true measure of success is the ratio between what we might have done and what we might have been on the one hand, and the thing we have made and the things we have made of ourselves on the other.
H. G. Wells

An artist must never be a prisoner. Prisoner? An artist should never be a prisoner of himself, prisoner of style, prisoner of reputation, prisoner of success, etc.
Henri Matisse

My success and my misfortunes, the bright and the dark days I have gone through, everything has proved to me that in this world, either physical or moral, good comes out of evil just as well as evil comes out of good.
Giacomo Casanova

The ladder of success in Hollywood is usually a press agent, actor, director, producer, leading man and you are a star if you sleep with each of them in that order. Crude, but true.

Hedy Lamarr

Success in training the boy depends largely on the Scoutmaster's own personal example.
Robert Baden-Powell

That's the definition of 'success' for the modern Democrat Party. As many people dependent on government as possible is the objective.
Rush Limbaugh

Remember you will not always win. Some days, the most resourceful individual will taste defeat. But there is, in this case, always tomorrow - after you have done your best to achieve success today.
Maxwell Maltz

Failure is the condiment that gives success its flavor.
Truman Capote

Success is only meaningful and enjoyable if it feels like your own.
Michelle Obama

Men judge us by the success of our efforts. God looks at the efforts themselves.
Charlotte Bronte

The power of fortune is confessed only by the miserable, for the happy impute all their success to prudence or merit.

Jonathan Swift

I have always been pushed by the negative. The apparent failure of a play sends me back to my typewriter that very night, before the reviews are out. I am more compelled to get back to work than if I had a success.
Tennessee Williams

We are taught to consume. And that's what we do. But if we realized that there really is no reason to consume, that it's just a mind set, that it's just an addiction, then we wouldn't be out there stepping on people's hands climbing the corporate ladder of success.
River Phoenix

But while success and failure depend on conditions, the mind neither waxes nor wanes.
Bodhidharma

No one can possibly achieve any real and lasting success or 'get rich' in business by being a conformist.

J. Paul Getty

Think of success as a game of chance in which you have control over the odds. As you begin to master concepts in personal achievement, you are increasing your odds of achieving success.
Bo Bennett

Success is about enjoying what you have and where you are, while pursuing achievable goals.
Bo Bennett

From success you get a lot of things, but not that great inside thing that love brings you.
Samuel Goldwyn

I want anyone who believes in life, liberty, pursuit of happiness to succeed. And I want any force, any person, any element of an overarching Big Government that would stop your success, I want that organization, that element or that person to fail. I want you to succeed.
Rush Limbaugh

Don't think of it as failure. Think of it as time-released success.
Robert Orben

I hate the idea of success robbing you of your private life.
Paul McCartney

I don't think about my previous success. I'm happy that the work I've done has been very successful.
Aaliyah

Success is a journey, not a destination. The doing is often more important than the outcome.

Arthur Ashe

Nobody travels on the road to success without a puncture or two.
Navjot Singh Sidhu

The first requisite for success is the ability to apply your physical and mental energies to one problem incessantly without growing weary.
Charles Caleb Colton

Constant success shows us but one side of the world adversity brings out the reverse of the picture.
Charles Caleb Colton

Success and failure are equally disastrous.
Tennessee Williams

Luxury is the wolf at the door and its fangs are the vanities and conceits germinated by success. When an artist learns this, he knows where the danger is.
Tennessee Williams

Success isn't permanent and failure isn't fatal.
Mike Ditka

Whether in success or in failure, I'm proud of every single movie I've ever directed.
Steven Spielberg

Ambition is the path to success. Persistence is the vehicle you arrive in.   **Bill Bradley**

Anyone who wants to sell you overnight success or wealth is not interested in your success they are interested in your money.
Bo Bennett

Everything you need for better future and success has already been written. And guess what? All you have to do is go to the library.
Henri Frederic Amiel

The two most important requirements for major success are: first, being in the right place at the right time, and second, doing something about it.
Ray Kroc

Singleness of purpose is one of the chief essentials for success in life, no matter what may be one's aim.
John D. Rockefeller

Success - keeping your mind awake and your desire asleep.
Walter Scott

Think of yourself as on the threshold of unparalleled success. A whole, clear, glorious life lies before you. Achieve! Achieve!
Andrew Carnegie

Our purpose in Vietnam is to prevent the success of aggression. It is not conquest, it is not empire, it is not foreign bases, it is not domination. It is, simply put, just to prevent the forceful conquest of South Vietnam by North Vietnam.
Lyndon B. Johnson

Talent alone won't make you a success. Neither will being in the right place at the right time, unless you are ready. The most important question is: 'Are your ready?'
Johnny Carson

Like so many American families, our families weren't asking for much. They didn't begrudge anyone else's success or care that others had much more than they did... in fact, they admired it.
Michelle Obama

Success is the sum of small efforts - repeated day in and day out.
Robert Collier

Most success springs from an obstacle or failure. I became a cartoonist largely because I failed in my goal of becoming a successful executive.
Scott Adams

Success is getting and achieving what you want. Happiness is wanting and being content with what you get.

Bernard Meltzer

On receiving from the people the sacred trust twice confided on my illustrious predecessor, and which he has discharged so faithfully and so well, I know that I can not expect to perform the arduous task with equal ability and success.
Martin Van Buren

The level of our success is limited only by our imagination and no act of kindness, however small, is ever wasted.
Aesop

I don't know what keeps me going. Sometimes I wonder... I think it's just pure perseverance and wanting to succeed and having that burning desire to always have success.
Tanya Tucker

Success should always be just beyond your grasp.
William Shatner

In the United States there's a Puritan ethic and a mythology of success. He who is successful is good. In Latin countries, in Catholic countries, a successful person is a sinner.
Umberto Eco

Success took me to her bosom like a maternal boa constrictor.

Noel Coward

Temporary success can be achieved in spite of lack of other fundamental qualities, but no advancements can be maintained without hard work.
William Feather

Honesty is the most single most important factor having a direct bearing on the final success of an individual, corporation, or product.
Ed McMahon

When success comes, people can try to trick you or take advantage of you.
Christina Aguilera

No man is a success in business unless he loves his work.
Florence Scovel Shinn

I was motivated by just thinking that if you had all this external success that everyone would love you and everything would be peaceful and wonderful.
Alanis Morissette

It's not just the 'Grammys' that I've pulled out of. I also pulled out of the English awards as well. The reason that I wanted to pull out was because I believe very much that the music industry as a whole is mainly concerned with material success.
Alanis Morissette

It is on our failures that we base a new and different and better success.
Havelock Ellis

Success is a consequence and must not be a goal.
Gustave Flaubert

Personal relationships are the fertile soil from which all advancement, all success, all achievement in real life grows.
Ben Stein

An actor's popularity is fleeting. His success has the life expectancy of a small boy who is about to look into a gas tank with a lighted match.
Fred Allen

Give me a couple of years, and I'll make that actress an overnight success.
Samuel Goldwyn

I'll tell you, there is nothing better in life than being a late bloomer. I believe that success can happen at any time and at any age.
Salma Hayek

You've achieved success in your field when you don't know whether what you're doing is work or play.
Warren Beatty

Success is survival.
Leonard Cohen

The appreciative smile, the chuckle, the soundless mirth, so important to the success of comedy, cannot be understood unless one sits among the audience and feels the warmth created by the quality of laughter that the audience takes home with it.
James Thurber

Your success depends mainly upon what you think of yourself and whether you believe in yourself.
William J. H. Boetcker

The distance between insanity and genius is measured only by success.
Bruce Feirstein

After a lifetime of working, raising families, and contributing to the success of this nation in countless other ways, senior citizens deserve to retire with dignity.
Charlie Gonzalez

There is much to be said for failure. It is much more interesting than success.
Max Beerbohm

To get down to the quick of it, respect motivates me - not success.
Hugh Jackman

Success is sweet and sweeter if long delayed and gotten through many struggles and defeats.
Amos Bronson Alcott

I believe in luck: how else can you explain the success of those you dislike?
Jean Cocteau

The will to persevere is often the difference between failure and success.
David Sarnoff

The most successful men in the end are those whose success is the result of steady accretion.
Alexander Graham Bell

Failure is simply the non-presence of success. But a fiasco is a disaster of mythic proportions.
Orlando Bloom

Let us realize that: the privilege to work is a gift, the power to work is a blessing, the love of work is success!
David O. McKay

I've stopped apologizing to myself for having this great period of success and financial acceptance.
Robert Plant

People fall forward to success.

Mary Kay Ash

Within the U.S., the Obama presidency will be mainly measured by the success or failure of his economic policies. And here, I fear, the monstrous stimulus package with which this administration stumbled out of the gate will prove to be Obama's Waterloo.
Camille Paglia

I define success as being comfortable with yourself and your life. And that is about as good as it gets, really.
Treat Williams

The person interested in success has to learn to view failure as a healthy, inevitable part of the process of getting to the top.
Joyce Brothers

Think little goals and expect little achievements. Think big goals and win big success.
David Joseph Schwartz

Why be a man when you can be a success?
Bertolt Brecht

I have no time for those who say there is no way Scotland could go it alone. I know first-hand the contribution Scotland and Scots make to Britain's success - so for me there's no question about whether Scotland could be an independent nation.

David Cameron

Hopefully I'll continue to have the success I've had.
Tiger Woods

The thing you don't dream about as a kid is all the peripheral stuff that comes with success.
Tiger Woods

The reward of art is not fame or success but intoxication: that is why so many bad artists are unable to give it up.
Jean Cocteau

Providence has nothing good or high in store for one who does not resolutely aim at something high or good. A purpose is the eternal condition of success.
Thornton Wilder

We are a people that have always celebrated other people's success so long as we always had the opportunity to meet that success ourselves. That is the American nature. That is the American character. That is one of the things that makes us different from the rest of the world. And I'm afraid we could lose that or are on the verge of losing that.
Marco Rubio

If you want to be truly successful invest in yourself to get the knowledge you need to find your unique

factor. When you find it and focus on it and persevere your success will blossom.
Sidney Madwed

I hate to be a failure. I hate and regret the failure of my marriages. I would gladly give all my millions for just one lasting marital success.
J. Paul Getty

The prospect of success in achieving our most cherished dream is not without its terrors. Who is more deprived and alone than the man who has achieved his dream?
Brendan Francis

If God has made the world a perfect mechanism, He has at least conceded so much to our imperfect intellect that in order to predict little parts of it, we need not solve innumerable differential equations, but can use dice with fair success.
Max Born

I'm an eternal realist and the success rate for being an actor is pretty low.
Tom Hiddleston

Success has nothing to do with what you gain in life or accomplish for yourself. It's what you do for others.
Danny Thomas

For someone who's had the level of success I've had, there's been very little critical review of my work, which is pretty fascinating.
Billy Corgan

Rock and Roll is still asking people like me to live up to the old guard's concept of what success is but it doesn't mean anything.
Billy Corgan

There could be no honor in a sure success, but much might be wrested from a sure defeat.
Ann Landers

It was so draining. Going to parties to rub elbows with so-and-so and act like it's no big deal, when really all I was doing was hoping I'd have the success they had.
Katy Perry

I'm either going to go completely mental, completely bankrupt, or have the best success of my life.
Katy Perry

One fails forward toward success.
Charles Kettering

We're not uncomfortable with it, and we've already been through enough of the music business where I'm not really worried that commercial success is going to in some way - we're already past saving, you know what I mean? It's too late for us.

Jerry Garcia

Success represents the 1% of your work which results from the 99% that is called failure.
Soichiro Honda

The worst part of success is to try finding someone who is happy for you.
Bette Midler

The making of friends who are real friends, is the best token we have of a man's success in life.
Edward Everett Hale

Some of the best lessons we ever learn are learned from past mistakes. The error of the past is the wisdom and success of the future.
Dale Turner

Permanent success cannot be achieved except by incessant intellectual labour, always inspired by the ideal.
Sarah Bernhardt

I worked half my life to be an overnight success, and still it took me by surprise.
Jessica Savitch

The danger of success is that it makes us forget the world's dreadful injustice.
Jules Renard

For a good 10 to 12 years, I was working non-stop and I wasn't really enjoying my success.
Shania Twain

I think all those people I did stories about measured their own success by the joy their work was giving them.
Charles Kuralt

The media says that equality for women has arrived, but if you look around, you still don't see girls playing guitars and having success with it.
Joan Jett

The keys to brand success are self-definition, transparency, authenticity and accountability.
Simon Mainwaring

Refuse to accept the belief that your professional relevance, career success or financial security turns on the next update on the latest technology. Sometimes it's good to put the paddle down and just let the canoe glide.
Simon Mainwaring

The secret of success is to be in harmony with existence, to be always calm to let each wave of life wash us a little farther up the shore.
Cyril Connolly

Indeed I regard the enduring support which I have received over the years from all sections of the community in Ballymena as being more than sufficient recognition for any success which I may have achieved as an actor.
Liam Neeson

No one is guaranteed happiness. You can pursue it, but if you happen to find success along the way on that road to happiness, Conservatives believe you should not be demonized or penalized for it.
Glenn Beck

Success is never final, but failure can be.
Bill Parcells

I am highly offended by the total lack of acknowledgement of my contribution to Laker success.

Kareem Abdul-Jabbar

If not for the success that medicine has made, I might be part of a much different story right now.
Kareem Abdul-Jabbar

Democrats believe in reigniting the American dream by removing barriers to success and building ladders of opportunity for all, so everyone can succeed.
Nancy Pelosi

People are beginning to see that the first requisite to success in life is to be a good animal.
Herbert Spencer

Success is achieved by developing our strengths, not by eliminating our weaknesses.
Marilyn vos Savant

I cannot give you the formula for success, but I can give you the formula for failure - which is: Try to please everybody.
Herbert Bayard Swope

Hope... is the companion of power, and the mother of success for who so hopes has within him the gift of miracles.
Samuel Smiles

When a small child, I thought that success spelled happiness. I was wrong, happiness is like a butterfly which appears and delights us for one brief moment, but soon flits away.
Anna Pavlova

Success makes men rigid and they tend to exalt stability over all the other virtues tired of the effort of willing they become fanatics about conservatism.
Walter Lippmann

Failure is a part of success.
Hank Aaron

Sometimes people take it for granted that they had success, especially nowadays when you have instant stardom. A lot of people feel entitlement and nobody is entitled to anything.
Donny Osmond

America's wealth comes from the efforts of people striving for success. Take away their incentive with badmouthing success and you take away the wealth that helps us take care of the needy.
Thomas Peterffy

You have reached the pinnacle of success as soon as you become uninterested in money, compliments, or publicity.
Thomas Wolfe

It's ironic that at age 32, at probably the greatest moment of my career, with The Godfather having such an enormous success, I wasn't even aware of it, because I was somewhere else under the deadline again.
Francis Ford Coppola

Success is usually the culmination of controlling failure.
Sylvester Stallone

Success is just being happy. And I try so many different things. I do a lot of different things. Because

I think God has helped me to love myself. I know who God is, and I love God.
Herschel Walker

The road to success is always under construction.
Arnold Palmer

Success for me its to raise happy, healthy human beings.
Kelly LeBrock

My success was due to good luck, hard work, and support and advice from friends and mentors. But most importantly, it depended on me to keep trying after I had failed.
Mark Warner

A minute's success pays the failure of years.
Robert Browning

I believe there are three keys to success. For me it is keeping my priorities in order: It's my faith and my family, and then the business.
Kathy Ireland

Without an open-minded mind, you can never be a great success.
Martha Stewart

You've got to eat while you dream. You've got to deliver on short-range commitments, while you

develop a long-range strategy and vision and implement it. The success of doing both. Walking and chewing gum if you will. Getting it done in the short-range, and delivering a long-range plan, and executing on that.
Jack Welch

There's no right or wrong, success or failure.
Miley Cyrus

I always say be humble but be firm. Humility and openness are the key to success without compromising your beliefs.
George Hickenlooper

I think people often confuse success with fame and stardom.
Brenda Blethyn

Well, certainly one of the ironies of the success of affirmative action is that the middle class within the black community no longer lives within 'black community' by and large.
Henry Louis Gates

The historical basis for the gap between the black middle class and underclass shows that ending discrimination, by itself, would not eradicate black poverty and dysfunction. We also need intervention to promulgate a middle-class ethic of success among the

poor, while expanding opportunities for economic betterment.
Henry Louis Gates

I sort of understood that when I first started: that you shouldn't repeat a success. Very often you're going to, and maybe the first time you do, it works. And you love it. But then you're trapped.
Jack Nicholson

The very first step towards success in any occupation is to become interested in it.
William Osler

About the only problem with success is that it does not teach you how to deal with failure.
Tommy Lasorda

Positive thinking is the key to success in business, education, pro football, anything that you can mention. I go out there thinking that I'm going to complete every pass.
Ron Jaworski

You really have to work hard and apply yourself and by applying yourself and working hard and being diligent, you can achieve success.
Julie Benz

Success breeds complacency. Complacency breeds failure. Only the paranoid survive.

Andy Grove

Success is like a liberation or the first phrase of a love story.
Jeanne Moreau

So many stars lose their way, and with success become more neurotic, not less so.
Francesca Annis

It is a mistake to suppose that men succeed through success they much oftener succeed through failures. Precept, study, advice, and example could never have taught them so well as failure has done.
Samuel Smiles

Success breeds success.
Mia Hamm

I always think I'm the Tom Cruise of music - a lot of success and fans, but no critics, darling.
Jon Bon Jovi

Like the British Constitution, she owes her success in practice to her inconsistencies in principle.
Thomas Hardy

Well, success does not mean doing well.
Shirley MacLaine

Remember, I come from such an excessively overdone, red-carpet place called Hollywood. So I'm used to people blowing up their success in ways that are far above and beyond the truth.
Shirley MacLaine

Although in skating you compete with other people, anyone who achieves a certain level of success is first and foremost competing against themselves. And for me the idea that I could always do better, learn more, learn faster, is something that came from skating. But I carried that with me for the rest of my life.
Vera Wang

Success and failure are both part of life. Both are not permanent.
Shahrukh Khan

Success can't be forced.
Loretta Young

I'd rather have huge success and huge failures than travel in the middle of the road.
Kevyn Aucoin

Fathers and mothers have lost the idea that the highest aspiration they might have for their children is for them to be wise... specialized competence and success are all that they can imagine.
Allan Bloom

Many individuals are doing what they can. But real success can only come if there is a change in our societies and in our economics and in our politics.
David Attenborough

Being a part of success is more important than being personally indispensable.
Pat Riley

Success cannot come from standstill men. Methods change and men must change with them.
James Cash Penney

I wanted to highlight that whole dreadful process in book publishing that 'nothing succeeds like success.'
Doris Lessing

The secret of our success is that we never, never give up.
Wilma Mankiller

I think the success of democracy is not really police security it's the presence of a broad middle class. The stronger the middle class of a people is, the less you have to worry about one group coming in and exploiting the democratic process for its own ends.
King Abdullah II

I wish I could just go tell all the young women I work with, all these fabulous women, 'Believe in yourself and negotiate for yourself. Own your own success.' I

wish I could tell that to my daughter. But it's not that simple.
Sheryl Sandberg

It's so interesting how success hits people and how they react to it.
John Mayer

I get hired by companies to hack into their systems and break into their physical facilities to find security holes. Our success rate is 100% we've always found a hole.
Kevin Mitnick

You've got to work hard for your success and you've got to have a steady presence. That's the secret.
Kid Rock

Success always necessitates a degree of ruthlessness. Given the choice of friendship or success, I'd probably choose success.
Sting

One of the rewards of success is freedom, the ability to do whatever you like.
Sting

I want to swim in both directions at once. Desire success, court failure.
Alan Rickman

Breast cancer deaths in America have been declining for more than a decade. Much of that success is due to early detection and better treatments for women. I strongly encourage women to get a mammogram.
Larry Craig

I have a tendency to sabotage relationships I have a tendency to sabotage everything. Fear of success, fear of failure, fear of being afraid. Useless, good-for-nothing thoughts.
Michael Buble

Young man, the secret of my success is that an early age I discovered that I was not God.
Oliver Wendell Holmes, Jr.

The framers of the Constitution were so clear in the federalist papers and elsewhere that they felt an independent judiciary was critical to the success of the nation.
Sandra Day O'Connor

The great dream merchant Disney was a success because make-believe was what everyone seemed to need in a spiritually empty land.
Arthur Erickson

Well, I think that there's a very thin dividing line between success and failure. And I think if you start a business without financial backing, you're likely to go the wrong side of that dividing line.

Richard Branson

Rockefeller once explained the secret of success. 'Get up early, work late - and strike oil.'
Joey Adams

I don't dwell on success. Maybe that's one reason I'm successful.
Calvin Klein

Success consists of getting up just one more time than you fall.
Oliver Goldsmith

We need to accept that we won't always make the right decisions, that we'll screw up royally sometimes - understanding that failure is not the opposite of success, it's part of success.
Arianna Huffington

Every soldier must know, before he goes into battle, how the little battle he is to fight fits into the larger picture, and how the success of his fighting will influence the battle as a whole.
Bernard Law Montgomery

You know, I start with the assumption that -or with, with the belief that this president has to succeed. We all have an enormous amount of capital invested in his success. His success is the country's success.
Michael Bloomberg

I think the idea that you know who your inner self is on a daily basis, because... you know. What's good for you 25 years ago may not be good for you now. So, to keep in touch with that, I think that's the first ingredient for success. Because if you're a successful human being, everything else is gravy, I think.
Whoopi Goldberg

Without failure there is no sweetness in success. There's no understanding of it.
Glenn Beck

In most things success depends on knowing how long it takes to succeed.
Charles de Montesquieu

Islam is a religion of success. Unlike Christianity, which has as its main image, in the west at least, a man dying in a devastating, disgraceful, helpless death.
Karen Armstrong

We moved into the back, made it into a little 50s sitting room and started to sell the records. We had an immediate success. For one thing, these Teddy Boys were thrilled to buy the records.
Vivienne Westwood

I don't think success is harmful, as so many people say. Rather, I believe it indispensable to talent, if for nothing else than to increase the talent.
Jeanne Moreau

Obama is capable - as evidenced by his first-term success with health care reform. But mandate-building requires humility, a trait not easily associated with him.
Ron Fournier

I always think, when there's stuff that people don't like, I always say that if I have another success, I'll enjoy it more, but you don't really.
Danny Boyle

I think that the reason for my success is that I am really not aspirational. I am inspirational in that the people at home feel like they can really relate to me.
Rosie O'Donnell

American inventiveness and the desire to build developed because we were guaranteed the right to own our success.
Rand Paul

Nothing succeeds like the appearance of success.
Christopher Lasch

It is not the possession of truth, but the success which attends the seeking after it, that enriches the seeker and brings happiness to him.
Max Planck

Success isn't everything but it makes a man stand straight.
Lillian Hellman

There's more to life than success, and if you can try to be more well-rounded, you'll be able to enjoy your success more. It won't own you or control you.
Ricky Williams

In New York, everyone's desperate for success, desperate for money and desperate to be accepted, but in London they're more laid back about things like that.
David Bailey

Success is always something completely different to people. I feel like I've succeeded, if I'm doing something that makes me happy and I'm not lying to anybody. I'm not doing that now, so I feel really good about myself.
Kristen Stewart

This weird thing happens when you're in a movie that has some level of success. People start offering you all kinds of things, and they just expect you to do them

because they'll be good for your career. It's not about the project's integrity or anything like that.
Kristen Stewart

One measure of your success will be the degree to which you build up others who work with you. While building up others, you will build up yourself.
James E. Casey

Money does not guarantee success.
Jose Mourinho

All those who are around me are the bridge to my success, so they are all important.
Manny Pacquiao

For an actress to be a success, she must have the face of a Venus, the brains of a Minerva, the grace of Terpsichore, the memory of a MaCaulay, the figure of Juno, and the hide of a rhinoceros.
Ethel Barrymore

The art of effective listening is essential to clear communication, and clear communication is necessary to management success.
James Cash Penney

The most absurd and reckless aspirations have sometimes led to extraordinary success.
Luc de Clapiers

The best revenge in the world is success.
Suge Knight

An entrepreneur assumes the risk and is dedicated and committed to the success of whatever he or she undertakes.
Victor Kiam

Entrepreneurs are risk takers, willing to roll the dice with their money or reputation on the line in support of an idea or enterprise. They willingly assume responsibility for the success or failure of a venture and are answerable for all its facets.
Victor Kiam

Do business managers have a commitment to anything more than the success of their company and to making money? It would be hard to say that they do. Indeed, many business leaders deny that there is any conflict between self-interest and the interests of all.
Peter Singer

Eventually, with success, I started to feel more and more isolated - like I didn't have a community of artists.
Joni Mitchell

When you grow up in the music industry, trying to be Britney Spears because that's what sells records and then you realize, 'All I have to do is be myself? I

should have thought of that a long time ago,' it feels good to have success come from what's actually inside of you.
Jessica Simpson

I'm sure not afraid of success and I've learned not to be afraid of failure. The only thing I'm afraid of now is of being someone I don't like much.
Anna Quindlen

I was very clear that I wanted to keep 'Thor' out of the rest of the Marvel universe for no less than the first six issues. And the success of the book, I think, speaks well to that decision.
J. Michael Straczynski

Liberals tend to put the onus of your success on society and conservatives on you and your family.
Dennis Prager

I planned my success. I knew it was going to happen.

Erykah Badu

I've learned that success comes in a very prickly package. Whether you choose to accept it or not is up to you.
Sandra Bullock

Success and the art of making music are two different things for me.

Norah Jones

With everything that is complex, we learn. If you don't learn, then it's an utter and abject failure. If you do learn, and you're able to apply that to the next situation, then you take away a measure of success.
Benjamin Carson

Education is a fundamental principle of what made America a success. We can't afford to throw any young people away.
Benjamin Carson

I am not fighting for success, just to get more beauty out of myself and share it with more people.
Ben Okri

People think your success is just a matter of having a pretty face. But it's easy to be chewed up and spat out. You've got to stay ahead of the game to be able to stay in it.
Kate Moss

To do a common thing uncommonly well brings success.
Henry J. Heinz

The only question to ask yourself is, how much are you willing to sacrifice to achieve this success?
Larry Flynt

Your chances of success in any undertaking can always be measured by your belief in yourself.
Robert Collier

So much of a professional athlete's success depends upon not necessarily the play itself but how he deals with... always saying how you deal with good, is just as important as how you deal with bad.
Brett Favre

The secret of success is sincerity.
Jean Giraudoux

But no nation can base its survival and development on luck and prayers alone while its leadership fritters away every available opportunity for success and concrete achievement.
Ibrahim Babangida

And in reality, I don't think it's a real documentary. It's more a story of her life. It's a story of survival. It's a story of the time in which she lived. The story of success and failure.
Maximilian Schell

Success is following the pattern of life one enjoys most.
Al Capp

For marriage to be a success, every woman and every man should have her and his own bathroom. The end.

Catherine Zeta-Jones

I've had great success being a total idiot.
Jerry Lewis

The film is not a success until it makes money. It's only good when there's a dollar figure attached to the box office.
John Cusack

No one ever attains success by simply doing what is required of him.
Charles Kendall Adams

They thought I was a success as soon as I started paying the bills.
Mahalia Jackson

The hardest thing to find in life is balance - especially the more success you have, the more you look to the other side of the gate. What do I need to stay grounded, in touch, in love, connected, emotionally balanced? Look within yourself.
Celine Dion

My father was an immigrant who literally walked across Europe to get out of Russia. He fought in World War I. He was wounded in action. My father was a

great success even though he never had money. He was a very determined man, a great role model.
Arlen Specter

We create success or failure on the course primarily by our thoughts.
Gary Player

I feel lucky because I was a nerd, which I talk about in the book, but I had academic success, so through that, because that's what my parents put a great deal of value on, I had a great childhood because I sort of fulfilled the expectations of being good at school.
Mindy Kaling

My success just evolved from working hard at the business at hand each day.
Johnny Carson

The road to success is filled with women pushing their husbands along.
Thomas R. Dewar

Sometimes success will get in the way of maturity - at least temporarily.
Ricky Williams

Anytime you play a team sport, the success of the team really makes everything better. It's nice.
Ricky Williams

I had a lot of success from the start. I never really was tested for long periods of time. I got my first professional job while I was a senior in college. I signed with the William Morris Agency before I graduated.
Denzel Washington

Which is - you know, like check it out, I'm pretty young, I'm only about 40 years old. I still have maybe another four decades of work left in me. And it's exceedingly likely that anything I write from this point forward is going to be judged by the world as the work that came after the freakish success of my last book, right?
Elizabeth Gilbert

I should just put it bluntly, because we're all sort of friends here now - it's exceedingly likely that my greatest success is behind me. Oh, so Jesus, what a thought! You know that's the kind of thought that could lead a person to start drinking gin at nine o'clock in the morning, and I don't want to go there.
Elizabeth Gilbert

When somebody has an enormous success in this culture, people start asking two questions, which are 'What are you doing now?' and 'How are you going to beat that?' And I have to say, I love the assumption that your intention is to beat yourself constantly - that you're in battle against yourself.
Elizabeth Gilbert

My career started young and I was really ambitious, and then I had success and I hung out with people who were much older. I think I might have been temporally misplaced, so I thought I was 40. It was a premature midlife crisis.
Elizabeth Gilbert

The only success worth one's powder was success in the line of one's idiosyncrasy... what was talent but the art of being completely whatever one happened to be?
Henry James

I believe success is preparation, because opportunity is going to knock on your door sooner or later but are you prepared to answer that?
Omar Epps

You'll never convince me there is a hopeless situation or there is any finality in any success or any failure.
Carlos Ghosn

The manic pursuit of success cost me everything I could love: my wife, my three children, some friends I would have liked to grow old with.
Sammy Davis, Jr.

The success of the Rat Pack or the Clan was due to the camaraderie, the three guys who work together and kid each other and love each other.

Sammy Davis, Jr.

Real success is not on the stage, but off the stage as a human being, and how you get along with your fellow man.
Sammy Davis, Jr.

Everyone has determination - it's a question of how you use it. Hers is based on power and success and conquering she doesn't care what she has to do or who gets hurt in the process. In that way we're very, very different.
Dannii Minogue

A lot of football success is in the mind. You must believe you are the best and then make sure that you are.
Bill Shankly

Muslims must believe that all power, success and victory comes from God alone.
Abu Bakar Bashir

Once you have a lot of success, you become a target in many ways.
Jennifer Lopez

Without Arthur's voice, I never would have enjoyed that success.
Paul Simon

A tragic irony of life is that we so often achieve success or financial independence after the chief reason for which we sought it has passed away.
Ellen Glasgow

There's not an instruction manual on how to deal with success, so you just have to rely on having great friends and a good team.
Bryan Adams

Success is measured by your discipline and inner peace.
Mike Ditka

The Occupy movement needs an organizing principle, and - just as the Tea Party did - it needs some actual measures of success. Choose one candidate whose agenda is squarely within that of the movement and make his or her electoral success a focal point.
Eliot Spitzer

In the end, you make your reputation and you have your success based upon credibility and being able to provide people who are really hungry for information what they want.
Brit Hume

You've got to ask! Asking is, in my opinion, the world's most powerful - and neglected - secret to success and happiness.
Percy Ross

Despite the success cult, men are most deeply moved not by the reaching of the goal but by the grandness of the effort involved in getting there - or failing to get there.
Max Lerner

My college degree was in theater. But the real reason, if I have any success in that milieu, so to speak, is because I spent a lot of years directing, I spent a lot of years behind the camera.
Alton Brown

Real success is being totally indulgent about your own trip. You put your blinders on about the garbage and go full speed ahead.
Betsey Johnson

Do something you really like, and hopefully it pays the rent. As far as I'm concerned, that's success.
Tom Petty

Success is more dangerous than failure, the ripples break over a wider coastline.
Graham Greene

Nearly all monster stories depend for their success on Jack killing the Giant, Beowulf or St. George slaying the Dragon, Harry Potter triumphing over the basilisk. That is their inner grammar, and the whole shape of the story leads towards it.

A. N. Wilson

I think you can have moderate success by copying something else, but if you really want to knock it out of the park, you have to do something different and take chances.
Lee Ann Womack

As you walk in God's divine wisdom, you will surely begin to see a greater measure of victory and good success in your life.
Joseph Prince

I didn't have a whole lot of success getting dates, I was always a bit of a geek.
Jim Davis

Success is the sweetest revenge.
Vanessa Williams

You can never be comfortable with your success, you've got to be paranoid you're going to lose it.
Lou Gerstner

Success needs no explanation. Failure does not have one that matters.
Jesse Jackson

It sounds cliche, but success is your friends, your family, what you do, and if you're happy when you wake up.

Michael Pitt

Success on any major scale requires you to accept responsibility... in the final analysis, the one quality that all successful people have... is the ability to take on responsibility.
Michael Korda

The only thing I can say about having this type of success is that you can get yourself in trouble because basically the world is set open for you. People will say yes to anything you ask, so it's basically down to you and what you want or need.
Bruce Springsteen

Your success story is a bigger story than whatever you're trying to say on stage. Success makes life easier. It doesn't make living easier.
Bruce Springsteen

It takes two to make a marriage a success and only one to make it a failure.
Herbert Samuel

The first principle of success is desire - knowing what you want. Desire is the planting of your seed.
Robert Collier

Don't be afraid of failure be afraid of petty success.
Maude Adams

Because after my first year I had a lot of success, took everybody by storm, came back the next year thought it was easy and didn't have near the season I had the previous year. It was kind of a wake-up call. And so, life goes on.

Brett Favre

Married couples who work together to build and maintain a business assume broad responsibilities. Not only is their work important to our local and national economies, but their success is central to the well-being of their families.

Melissa Bean

Hip-hop is more about attaining wealth. People respect success. They respect big. They don't even have to like your music. If you're big enough, people are drawn to you.

Jay-Z

True leadership lies in guiding others to success. In ensuring that everyone is performing at their best, doing the work they are pledged to do and doing it well.

Bill Owens

Modesty should be typical of the success of a champion.

Major Taylor

I will not be discouraged by failure I will not be elated by success.
Joseph Barber Lightfoot

Follow your passion. Nothing - not wealth, success, accolades or fame - is worth spending a lifetime doing things you don't enjoy.
Jonathan Sacks

Everybody loves success, but they hate successful people.
John McEnroe

By far the most important factor in the success or failure of any school, far more important than tests or standards or business-model methods of accountability, is simply attracting the best-educated, most exciting young people into urban schools and keeping them there.
Jonathan Kozol

There is never just one thing that leads to success for anyone. I feel it always a combination of passion, dedication, hard work, and being in the right place at the right time.
Lauren Conrad

Philanthropy is the thing that I am really excited about, and having success means I can do more.
Will.i.am

There is no scientific answer for success. You can't define it. You've simply got to live it and do it.
Anita Roddick

The secret to success is to own nothing, but control everything.
Nelson Rockefeller

It's the quality of the ordinary, the straight, the square, that accounts for the great stability and success of our nation. It's a quality to be proud of. But it's a quality that many people seem to have neglected.
Gerald R. Ford

We do not celebrate people who have made success out of serious hard work.
Iain Duncan Smith

Kids are meant to believe that their stepping stone to massive money is 'The X Factor.' Luck is great, but most of life is hard work. We do not celebrate people who have made success out of serious hard work.
Iain Duncan Smith

The problem with being British... I don't know if it's me being British or being raised a strict Catholic, but you never really enjoy success.
Danny Boyle

When humor can be made to alternate with melancholy, one has a success, but when the same things are funny and melancholic at the same time, it's just wonderful.
Francois Truffaut

Success makes you less intimidated by things.
Nate Silver

People still don't appreciate how ephemeral success is.

Nate Silver

I think that the entertainment industry itself has a history of chasing success. Any time a hit product comes out, all the other companies start chasing after that success and trying to recreate it by putting out similar products. **Shigeru Miyamoto**

It would be a joy for me if someone who was working with me became a big success.
Shigeru Miyamoto

In America, as opposed to the old country, success was based on merit.
Rand Paul

But I like not these great success of yours for I know how jealous are the gods.
Herodotus

I think the measure of your success to a certain extent will be the amount of things written about you that aren't true.
Cybill Shepherd

Success means having the courage, the determination, and the will to become the person you believe you were meant to be.
George A. Sheehan

I haven't deliberately set out to play the blonde bombshell in my movies. In fact, it's probably been quite the opposite. After the success of The Mask, I wasn't offered all that many blonde bombshell parts, to be honest. I think people believed from the beginning that I could actually walk and talk at the same time.
Cameron Diaz

Yes I have made a lot of money and I have a lot of respect, my films have done well, and I know there are loads of loads of people who look up to me and really love me. I really just thought this is like a strange dream. I have never thought this is a success - I don't have a standard.
Shahrukh Khan

All of us are born for a reason, but all of us don't discover why. Success in life has nothing to do with what you gain in life or accomplish for yourself. It's what you do for others.

Danny Thomas

My own early experiences in war led me to suspect the value of discipline, even in that sphere where it is so often regarded as the first essential for success.
Herbert Read

When people stand up and talk about the great success that the EU has been, I'm not sure anybody saying it really believes it themselves anymore.
Nigel Farage

I didn't have any success in show business until I was 30 to 31 years of age.
Adam Carolla

The NFL has been an amazing page in this chapter of my life. I pray that all successive adventures offer me the same potential for growth, success and most importantly fun.
Ricky Williams

As my father used to tell me, the only true sign of success in life is being able to do for a living that which makes you happy.
Al Yankovic

Am I coasting on some early success? Yeah. It was a good lucky break for me. But I would rather earn my way back again than simply conform to what people are expecting.

Liz Phair

One goes through school, college, medical school and one's internship learning little or nothing about goodness but a good deal about success.
Ashley Montagu

The secrets of success are a good wife and a steady job. My wife told me.
Howard Nemerov

Hollywood... a city I was to come back to time and again, in sickness and in health, in success and in failure, with anticipation and with dread.
Dirk Benedict

But I think it's more normal for my team to have no success than it is to win two consecutive European cups.
Jose Mourinho

I'm not a defender of old or new football managers. I believe in good ones and bad ones, those that achieve success and those that don't.
Jose Mourinho

I suppose your security is your success and your key to success is your fine palate.
Gordon Ramsay

I've had a lot of success I've had failures, so I learn from the failure.
Gordon Ramsay

Lesson from Pataki's success is: Use the political moment.
Andrew Cuomo

I realise that I do not change the course of history. I am an actor, I do a movie, that's the end of it. You have to realise we are just clowns for hire. After I had success it was great, at first, not to worry about money. It was on my mind when I was growing up.
Leonardo DiCaprio

I rejected the notion that my race or sex would bar my success in life.
Constance Baker Motley

Success depends almost entirely on how effectively you learn to manage the game's two ultimate adversaries: the course and yourself.
Jack Nicklaus

I'm glad that my parents missed one thing that was really unbelievable. They saw me hit this great success. It was a blast and we had a lot of laughs. And it was just an amazing time. They passed away. And then after I got, you know, famous, all these haters came out of nowhere.
Dane Cook

The one thing that makes me feel super lucky about my financial success is that I have a housekeeper.
Gwen Stefani

If I wasn't even famous or had any success, I would still wake up and put tons of make-up on, and put on a cool outfit. That's always been who I've been my whole life, so that's never gonna change. I love fashion. I love getting dressed up. I love Halloween, too.
Gwen Stefani

Success consists in being successful, not in having potential for success. Any wide piece of ground is the potential site of a palace, but there's no palace till it's built.
Fernando Pessoa

The quick success was a bit strange to get used to.
Fiona Apple

In a way, a certain amount of self-criticism is a good thing, because it keeps you humble. Realizing that no matter what success you've achieved, you can still make enemies makes you humble, too.
Lynn Johnston

Success is the necessary misfortune of life, but it is only to the very unfortunate that it comes early.
Anthony Trollope

Success is not in never failing, but rising everytime you fall!
Jonathan Taylor Thomas

I don't think about financial success as the measurement of my success.
Christie Hefner

Excess is success.
Roberto Cavalli

Sometimes, because of my success, I am afraid that I was not a good father. With the first two I was too strong, and with the other three I was too weak.
Roberto Cavalli

I feel like a hostage to fortune. Not that I am complaining. I wanted to play the role. But in truth I didn't think the show would be such a success. OK, I thought it would fail. Not because it was bad. I was confident it was good, but plenty of good things just sort of wither on the vine.
Hugh Laurie

I admit I can't shake the idea that there is virtue in suffering, that there is a sort of psychic economy, whereby if you embrace success, happiness and comfort, these things have to be paid for.
Hugh Laurie

It's absolutely essential that we have the same safeguards that straight couples do. But I want more than a 50 percent chance of success. I don't want to emulate that.
George Michael

I have more love, success, and security than I could ever dream of.
George Michael

I see nothing wrong with the human trait to desire. In fact, I consider it integral to our success mechanism. Becoming attached to what we desire is what causes the trouble. If you must have it in order to be happy, then you are denying the happiness of the here and now.
Peter McWilliams

Success is always temporary. When all is said and one, the only thing you'll have left is your character.
Vince Gill

When I meet successful people I ask 100 questions as to what they attribute their success to. It is usually the same: persistence, hard work and hiring good people.
Kiana Tom

With 'Believe' bringing really big success for me outside of the U.K. for the first time, it meant I have been touring around the world and that led to a gap

from the studio. I really feel like the gap has done me the world of good. Throughout that time I was able to collect songs that I really loved.
Katherine Jenkins

I have found no greater satisfaction than achieving success through honest dealing and strict adherence to the view that, for you to gain, those you deal with should gain as well.
Alan Greenspan

Like everybody, I have invested in things that have gone bad, because there's never any guarantee of success or profit when it comes to money.
Murray Walker

When everything happens to you when you're so young, you're very lucky, but by the same token, you're never going to have that same feeling again. The first time anything happens to you - your first love, your first success - the second one is never the same.
Lauren Bacall

We all know that Social Security is one of this country's greatest success stories in the 20th century.

Mitch McConnell

Enjoy failure and learn from it. You can never learn from success.

James Dyson

In the digital age of 'overnight' success stories such as Facebook, the hard slog is easily overlooked.
James Dyson

I went to America and got into a band, had success, had hits in Australia.
Rick Springfield

Yeah, ideally, I'd probably wish to be more anonymous. But scrutiny and success go together. And I want to be successful.
Paula Radcliffe

Well, I do feel that I carry the responsibility of representing my country wherever I am, and this responsibility came with the success that I had in last couple of years, not just myself but the whole group of tennis players that comes from Serbia. And athletes in general are, in this moment, the biggest ambassadors that our country has.
Novak Djokovic

There's a lot of blood, sweat, and guts between dreams and success.
Paul Bryant

I'm not sure anybody's ready to see me in a drama. And loving movies so much, I've seen a lot of comics try to make that transition too fast, and it can be

detrimental. And I don't think I've had as much success as I need in the comedy genre to open up those opportunities.
Seann William Scott

Being best is a false goal, you have to measure success on your own terms.
Damien Hirst

I want to make sure I don't interfere with the success of that team next year. I don't see any way I could go to practice like most of 'em do, and not hurt the team. I'd go nuts if I tried doing that.
Bear Bryant

The success of any great moral enterprise does not depend upon numbers.
William Lloyd Garrison

Team GB's success at the Beijing Olympics can, in part, be said to have been made in Manchester. For example, all the cycling medal winners trained at Manchester's velodrome, the National Cycling Centre.

Lucy Powell

For us political activists and candidates, the morning after any election is a mix of emotions - the personal and the immediate, the culmination of your own recent campaigning efforts and the fortunes of your

party and the success or otherwise of what you stand for and believe in.
Lucy Powell

I never expected any sort of success with 'Mockingbird'... I sort of hoped someone would like it enough to give me encouragement.
Harper Lee

I've learned it's always better to have a small percentage of a big success, than a hundred percent of nothing.
Art Linkletter

Though I had success in my research both when I was mad and when I was not, eventually I felt that my work would be better respected if I thought and acted like a 'normal' person.
John Forbes Nash

I don't think success arrives and you're suddenly happy. It's not like that. If people think that they'll be very disappointed.
Michael Hutchence

There is no middle ground in Hollywood you're a failure or you're a success. That mentality is wild.
Javier Bardem

I think the success of a talk show depends on how true it is to the personality of the person hosting it.

The shows I really admire, like 'Oprah' and 'Ellen,' are distinctively like their hosts, so I think my show will be successful only if we try to stay consistent to my own sense of myself.
Jane Pauley

Success will always be measured by the extent to which we serve the buying public.
James Cash Penney

Anyone who has to fight, even with the most modern weapons, against an enemy in complete command of the air, fights like a savage against modern European troops, under the same handicaps and with the same chances of success.
Erwin Rommel

To me, success is choice and opportunity.
Harrison Ford

Dullness in matters of government is a good sign, and not a bad one - in particular, dullness in parliamentary government is a test of its excellence, an indication of its success.
Walter Bagehot

The kind of theater that I do is sort of 'narrative realism,' which I think in the broadest sense is legitimate to say is mainstream. I mean, in a certain sense, Suzan-Lori's plays have had mainstream levels

of success. But Suzan-Lori is in some ways not a narrative realist.
Tony Kushner

I was, if you like, a successful schoolboy in that I had a degree of talent in all the required things that make you a success at school.
Damian Lewis

Success follows those adept at preserving the substance of the past by clothing it in the forms of the future.
Dee Hock

My store, Wine Library, outsells big national chains. How do you think we do it? It started with hustle. I always say that our success wasn't due to my hundreds of online videos about wine that went viral, but to the hours I spent talking to people online afterward, making connections and building relationships.
Gary Vaynerchuk

I always say that the real success of Wine Library wasn't due to the videos I posted, but to the hours I spent talking to people online afterward, making connections and building relationships.
Gary Vaynerchuk

Well, you can't be trying to achieve success of any kind in this business without accepting that there's going to be a flip side to it.
Jennifer Garner

Hosting a TV show is a full-time job in which success is defined by it never ending.
John Hodgman

I think success has no rules, but you can learn a great deal from failure.
Jean Kerr

Success in the majority of circumstances depends on knowing how long it takes to succeed.
Charles de Montesquieu

I'm starting to judge success by the time I have for myself, the time I spend with family and friends. My priorities aren't amending they're shifting.
Brendan Fraser

A sign now of success with a certain audience when you do a short comedy piece, anywhere, is that it gets on YouTube and gets around. It's always something you're thinking about unconsciously.
Andy Samberg

I mean, we are tribal by nature, and sometimes success and material wealth can divide and separate -

it's not a new philosophy I'm sharing - more than hardship, hardship tends to unify.
Colin Farrell

In my time and neighborhood (and in my soul) there was only one standard by which a woman measured success: did some man want her?
Jessamyn West

My definition of success is control.
Kenneth Branagh

If there is any secret to my success, I think it's that my characters are very real to me. I feel everything they feel, and therefore I think my readers care about them.
Sidney Sheldon

All business success rests on something labeled a sale, which at least momentarily weds company and customer.
Tom Peters

The whole secret to our success is being able to con ourselves into believing that we're going to change the world because statistically we are unlikely to do it.
Tom Peters

Failures to heroic minds are the stepping stones to success.
Thomas Chandler Haliburton

How easy to be amiable in the midst of happiness and success.
William Ellery Channing

Evolution acts slowly. Our psychological characteristics today are those that promoted reproductive success in the ancestral environment.
Keith Henson

To be associated with success is absolutely wonderful.

Roger Moore

Success depends in a very large measure upon individual initiative and exertion, and cannot be achieved except by a dint of hard work.
Anna Pavlova

Success produces confidence confidence relaxes industry, and negligence ruins the reputation which accuracy had raised.
Ben Jonson

I was trying to uphold what I thought feminism was as best I could by supporting women, by trying to create an opportunity to get women to get together, play music together and celebrate the fact that we are having great success making music on our own and together.
Sarah McLachlan

If there's no fire, there's no scream. If there's no scream, then no one hears you and no one comes to help you in the first place. The depth of my struggle has definitely determined the height of my success. To be able to teach my kids not just about success but about the struggle that comes with it.
R. Kelly

Put paying your dues and all that puts so much into being a success. You have an understanding of what it's about, being on your own for three or four years and living day to day on $3, or living in an apartment with no electricity.
Taylor Kitsch

For example, the equivalent of a woman being treated as a sex object is a man being treated as a success object.
Warren Farrell

The vampire was a complete change from the usual romantic characters I was playing, but it was a success.
Bela Lugosi

Success sometimes can really bite you in the shorts.
Donny Osmond

With success came an ever-growing burden of responsibility. I lived with a near-constant low-level

anxiety that I would make a mistake that would not only threaten my career, but also my brothers' - not to mention the livelihoods of many people who work with us or for us.
Donny Osmond

Such a faith would be fatal to my reason, to my liberty, and even to the success of my undertakings it would immediately transform me into a stupid slave, an instrument of the will and interests of others.
Mikhail Bakunin

I passionately believe that's it's not just what you say that counts, it's also how you say it - that the success of your argument critically depends on your manner of presenting it.
Alain de Botton

I was born with success. Lucky for me I am able to handle it. Also, I damn well deserve it!
Larry Hagman

Major success feels a bit like a coronation. Like I'd become a king. I was one of the most famous people in the world, loved and hated in equal measure. I couldn't see anything bad with it. It made me a happy person.
Larry Hagman

I think that everybody in the world, whatever colour or creed, has a jerk like JR in his or her family

somewhere. Whether it is a father, uncle, cousin or brother, everybody can identify with JR and that certainly had something to do with the success of 'Dallas.'
Larry Hagman

As his partner on this amazing journey, I can tell you Mitt Romney was not handed success. He built it.
Ann Romney

Sudden success in golf is like the sudden acquisition of wealth. It is apt to unsettle and deteriorate the character.
P. G. Wodehouse

I gave up a lot of things in exchange for my success.
Billy Sheehan

The success of Watermark surprised me. I never thought of music as something commercial it was something very personal to me.
Enya

That's the key to success, isn't it? It has to be fun.
Monica Seles

There's that unwritten schism that literary writers get all the awards and commercials writers get all the success.
Jodi Picoult

I think all of us certainly believed the statistics which said that probably 88% chance of mission success and maybe 96% chance of survival. And we were willing to take those odds.
Alan Shepard

You know, I can be the happiest man in the world with minimal record success.
Joe Nichols

I want to see success right away. And I want to never give up, never stop.
Joe Nichols

If you can go out with your live show and turn people on to that, where you have that fan base that's religious and they're going to come see you when you're in that town, once your radio success is gone and you're not a mainstream guy anymore you can still go out and play your shows.
Jason Aldean

A man desires praise that he may be reassured, that he may be quit of his doubting of himself he is indifferent to applause when he is confident of success.
Alec Waugh

Success is not assured, but America is resolute: this is the best chance for peace we are likely to see for

some years to come - and we are acting to help Israelis and Palestinians seize this chance.
Condoleezza Rice

When one has success, the answer is not to undo that success. It is to continue what has been done.
Charles Schumer

Writers, as they gain success, feel like outsiders because writers don't come together in real groups.
Anne Rice

First-person narrators is the way I know how to write a book with the greatest power and chance of artistic success.
Anne Rice

The first condition of success for the League of Nations is, therefore, a firm understanding between the British Empire and the United States of America and France and Italy that there will be no competitive building up of fleets or armies between them.
Arthur Henderson

One man has enthusiasm for 30 minutes, another for 30 days, but it is the man who has it for 30 years who makes a success of his life.
Edward B. Butler

It never made sense to me that someone would achieve any kind of success in show business, only to become a jerk.
Josh Radnor

You wanna know what scares people? Success. When you don't make moves and when you don't climb up the ladder, everybody loves you because you're not competition.
Nicki Minaj

Thought is the original source of all wealth, all success, all material gain, all great discoveries and inventions, and of all achievement.
Claude M. Bristol

It was a way out of poverty. It was a way to success. It was a way to education. And it was a way to a brighter day for me.
Little Richard

I raised five children. They all have different personalities. All of them have different issues, different levels of success. That was a learning experience for me.
T. D. Jakes

Look, if you ask a child, 'Would you rather have a fulfilled mother or a stay-at-home Sylvia Plath,' they'll pick Sylvia Plath every time. But I think it's really

important that children don't feel their parents' emotional lives depend on their success.
Ayelet Waldman

My literary success meant nothing to me.
Taylor Caldwell

I don't think success has changed us as people at all. We are the same lunatics that we were when this band first got going. We never see ourselves as being on a higher level than our fans.
Kirk Hammett

The key to sitcom success is miserable people. If you see a happy couple, it's just gone, like when Sam and Diane got together on Cheers.
Matthew Perry

If you can attribute your success entirely to your own mental effort, to your own attitude, to some spiritual essence that you have that is better than other people's, then that must feel pretty good.
Barbara Ehrenreich

The ever quickening advances of science made possible by the success of the Human Genome Project will also soon let us see the essences of mental disease. Only after we understand them at the genetic level can we rationally seek out appropriate therapies for such illnesses as schizophrenia and bipolar disease.

James D. Watson

Success is the person who year after year reaches the highest limits in his field.
Sparky Anderson

Success is important only to the extent that it puts one in a position to do more things one likes to do.
Sarah Caldwell

We were called The Toilets originally - we were flushed with success.
Mike Peters

Whenever I hear, 'It can't be done,' I know I'm close to success.
Michael Flatley

It was very clear to me in 1965, in Mississippi, that, as a lawyer, I could get people into schools, desegregate the schools, but if they were kicked off the plantations - and if they didn't have food, didn't have jobs, didn't have health care, didn't have the means to exercise those civil rights, we were not going to have success.
Marian Wright Edelman

Success is finding satisfaction in giving a little more than you take.
Christopher Reeve

We now live in a world where the only thing to have is success, but failure is marvelous. It's fertiliser, it's like living fertiliser, because you're forced on yourself.
Rupert Everett

Without imagination we can go nowhere. And imagination is not restricted to the arts. Every scientist I have met who has been a success has had to imagine.
Rita Dove

Everyone takes pause at 40. It's the age you have to assess everything in your life. It's the fictitious marker that's always coming up when you're young. The world really does look at you to kind of have it together by 40, and be successful by 40. Whatever success means.
Paul Feig

My formula for success is rise early, work late, and strike oil.
Paul Getty

Winning in Afghanistan is having a country that is stable enough to ensure that there is no safe haven for Al Qaida or for a militant Taliban that welcomes Al Qaida. That's really the measure of success for the United States.
Leon Panetta

I'm in the studio 24 hours a day. It's true that once you get a certain level of success, you become a target. Talk magazine should be ashamed of themselves.
Puff Daddy

In a balanced organization, working towards a common objective, there is success.
Arthur Helps

One is never ready for success. It consecrates and looses you at the same time.
Isabelle Adjani

It's both rebellion and conformity that attack you with success.
Amy Tan

I consider 'Dr. Horrible' a tremendous success. The fact that it won an Emmy I just think lends validity to what we were doing and the point we were trying to make: taking the power into someone else's hands and changing the world.
Nathan Fillion

But Big Oil and Big Coal have always been as skilled at propaganda as they are at mining and drilling. Like the tobacco industry before them, their success depends on keeping Americans stupid.
Jeff Goodell

To burn always with this hard, gem-like flame, to maintain this ecstasy, is success in life.
Walter Pater

For movies to get greenlit solely based on the success of other movies that have a lot of women in them? It's so ridiculous to me.
Kristen Wiig

I have decided to fight for my country, because we have build a success story in Guanajuato, with real results and more yet to come in the next two years.
Vicente Fox

Success tempts many to their ruin.
Phaedrus

Though I was excited about the Sojourner Truth play, it was not reassuring to think that my entire future might depend on the success of that one show.
Ethel Waters

The real end winner of NAFTA is going to be Mexico because we have the human capital. We have that resource that is vital to the success of the U.S. economy.
Vicente Fox

I feel true success comes from being able to work and the love for it.
Kiana Tom

People need to realise what real happiness and success is, because success as an actor is fleeting. You can be up there one day and gone the next.
Chuck Norris

My first attempt at a kiss was in fifth grade, but it didn't go so well. Later, I used Boyz II Men and Jodeci songs to come on to girls. I had more success.
John Legend

To this day, most people think of me as the fastest human. They don't really think me as a long jumper, although that's the event I had more success in.
Carl Lewis

There is no correlation between a childhood success and a professional athlete.
Carl Lewis

Mass communication, radio, and especially television, have attempted, not without success, to annihilate every possibility of solitude and reflection.
Eugenio Montale

I'd rather a young black actor read about success as opposed to how tough it was. I get these roles because I can act and that's it. Hopefully that's it.
Idris Elba

Success is hard in general for most women. We now have such busy lives, and we're told we can do everything - you know, we can have the relationship and the marriage and the kids and the career.
Cat Deeley

Four years of football are calculated to breed in the average man more of the ingredients of success in life than almost any academic course he takes.
Knute Rockne

I've had a lot of success over the years racing in New York, but the main point is that I feel the marathon is a different event, a lot more my event.
Paula Radcliffe

I did not become successful in my work through embracing or engaging in celebrity culture. I never signed away my privacy in exchange for success.
Steve Coogan

The success of Torn was a bit too much for me. I took a year off and was still scared to start the second album.
Natalie Imbruglia

Happy people are ignoramuses and glory is nothing else but success, and to achieve it one only has to be cunning.
Mikhail Lermontov

You may lose your wife, you may lose your dog, your mother may hate you. None of those things matter. What matters is that you achieve success and become free. Then you can do whatever you like.
Kevin O'Leary

Success is very ephemeral. You depend entirely on the desire of others, which makes it difficult to relax.
Eva Green

Success comes in waves.
Guy Pearce

I can't imagine wanting to be famous just for the sake of being famous. I think fame should come along with success, talent.
Kat Dennings

We just want to win. That's the bottom line. I think a lot of times people may become content with one championship or a little bit of success, but we don't really reflect on what we've done in the past. We focus on the present.
Derek Jeter

There are so few women in general who aren't completely threatened and confused by other women's success. It's very disappointing.
Sandra Bernhard

I don't understand why people whose entire lives or their corporate success depends on communication, and yet they are led on occasion by CEOs who cannot talk their way out of a paper bag and don't care to.
Frank Luntz

Sometimes success comes in ways you don't expect.
Ben Barnes

I think that my biggest attribute to any success that I have had is hard work. There really is no substitute for working hard.
Maria Bartiromo

You always pass failure on your way to success.
Mickey Rooney

Success listens only to applause. To all else it is deaf.

Elias Canetti

There's nothing so aphrodisiacal for a woman as money and success.
Wilbur Smith

The FHA's success provides strong evidence that government can and should play a role in the nation's mortgage finance system. It also demonstrates that although government intervention in the economy during the Great Recession was messy, things would have been a lot messier without it.

Mark Zandi

Whatever success I've had, I always like to top it.
Bernie Mac

We're born with success. It is only others who point
out our failures, and what they attribute to us as
failure.
Whoopi Goldberg

To win in Australia, for me, has to be the ultimate
success because the Aussies live for sport.
Ian Botham

A variety of national and international studies indicate
that the broad-based deployment of information
technology can have a substantial impact on our
nation's economic productivity and growth as well as
the educational and social success of our citizens.
Tim Holden

The fame of heroes owes little to the extent of their
conquests and all to the success of the tributes paid to
them.
Jean Genet

All these people who say success changes people well,
no, it just magnifies what's there.
Kevin Smith

Success is not a destination, but the road that you're on. Being successful means that you're working hard and walking your walk every day. You can only live your dream by working hard towards it. That's living your dream.
Marlon Wayans

Everyone applauds each other's success in Hollywood because they know how tough it is, but it really comes down fundamentally to the process.
Robert Rodriguez

My ambition was to stop waiting tables. That was how I measured success: finally, I was able to stop waiting tables, and I was able to pay the rent, and that was by being a stand-up comic. Not a very good stand-up comic, but good enough to make a living.
Graham Norton

I had come to the point when I realized it was unlikely that my film career was going to move beyond a certain level of role. And I was - because I had graphic instances of it - handicapped by the success of Star Trek. A director would say, 'I don't want Jean-Luc Picard in my movie' - and this was compounded by X-Men as well.
Patrick Stewart

More people on unemployment benefits is not success in America, fewer people on not because we kicked them off but because they have been able to get a job

in the private sector, because government got out of the way.
Scott Walker

I think most people believe success in government is how many fewer people are in government, not because you kick them off of benefits like unemployment but they've been able to control their own destiny because private sector employers have created more jobs.
Scott Walker

With the success of the last three or so years, when a lot of people start treating you differently, there's a danger that you may start to think of yourself differently. You rely on your friends to say, 'Hey, wake up!'
David Schwimmer

If the film is a hit then everyone shares the success. If it is going to be a disaster then it might as well be because of me, not because of somebody else.
Salman Khan

For the past few years, I was the more visible Asian performer, and I think it gave young girls a kind of role model showing it's possible to actually reach success doing movies.
Joan Chen

I came from a family where I felt great pressure to be financially successful, and I felt that staying in Chicago and doing theater, I was, in all likelihood, not going to find financial success.
David Schwimmer

For me, I don't feel it is a success in the career to be the pretty woman career success comes from being characters who tell us something about the truth.
Emmanuelle Beart

And really, the basis, I think, of achieving some success in what I want to do today comes from my mother's push to get me to read and to make something of myself from the standpoint of an education.
Sam Donaldson

If I can procure three hundred good substantial names of persons, or bodies, or institutions, I cannot fail to do well for my family, although I must abandon my life to its success, and undergo many sad perplexities and perhaps never see again my own beloved America.
John James Audubon

I've always been too hard on myself to behave like I've arrived or even to enjoy whatever success I've had. I've always envisioned myself higher than where I was and I still do. With each success I think, 'That's nice but I'm supposed to go there!'

Nicole Scherzinger

Success is a process, a quality of mind and way of being, an outgoing affirmation of life.
Alex Noble

For globalization to work for America, it must work for working people. We should measure the success of our economy by the breadth of our middle class, and the scope of opportunity offered to the poorest child to climb into that middle class.
John J. Sweeney

We had maybe the greatest success of any company that I know of in Paris, and after two or three years I wanted to do this same number that we did for PBS, so we did it and Paris had always considered us their darlings.
Katherine Dunham

It's hard for children's authors to be accepted when they try to write adult books. J.K. Rowling is the exception because people are so eager to read anything by her, but it took Judy Blume three or four tries before she had a success.
R. L. Stine

People of mediocre ability sometimes achieve outstanding success because they don't know when to quit. Most men succeed because they are determined to.

George Allen, Sr.

Women face enough pressures and challenges in a workplace that is still depressingly biased against a female's success. Add to that, the fact that the very thing many women I know find most rewarding (having kids) is now frowned upon.
Mika Brzezinski

Success is what you do with your ability. It's how you use your talent.
George Allen, Sr.

Other people's success spurs me on to do well and gives me motivation.
Nicholas Hoult

I've always known I would be a success, but I was surprised at the way it came.
Eva Gabor

Nothing reinforces a professional relationship more than enjoying success with someone.
Harold Ramis

The first myth of management is that it exists. The second myth of management is that success equals skill.
Robert Heller

I don't want to wake up and be bored. That's probably my greatest fear is to have nothing to do. What better job is there than to play quarterback for an NFL team, and certainly one that I've been on for a long time and had success with? I don't plan on giving it up any time soon.
Tom Brady

I thought doing reality TV would be the greatest success of my life or the biggest mistake.
Bethenny Frankel

Nothing fails like success nothing is so defeated as yesterday's triumphant Cause.
Phyllis McGinley

People repeat behaviour that leads to flooding their brains with pleasurable chemicals. The short-term reward loop acts over hours to years, and the long-term reproductive success loop over generations.
Keith Henson

Every success in limiting armaments is a sign that the will to achieve mutual understanding exists, and every such success thus supports the fight for international law and order.
Ludwig Quidde

Success is 99 percent failure.
Soichiro Honda

I have an idea of who I want to be, I have a vision of my own success.
Wiz Khalifa

Well, I believe that the depth of your struggle can determine the height of your success. I was inspired to come out of everything I've been through and end up in a place where I never thought that I would be.
R. Kelly

Success turns a lot of people off. I have a pretty solid sense of joy and respect that irritates people, and can irritate me, too.
Dave Matthews

I always envisioned myself being a rapper and being in the game and having success, but you never know what it feels like or how you're going to be when you're there.
Wiz Khalifa

Girlfriend and 100 Percent Fun were my two peeks, around '92 and '96. The reality is that the times I had the most media success, sold lots of records and played bigger shows, I had the least control of my own life.
Matthew Sweet

I was successful materially, but I know life is much more than worldly success. I saw all these blessings

God had given me. The way to give thanks is obedience to God.
Hakeem Olajuwon

Whenever you analyse anyone who has had any success and they're in the headlines, you will find they are human and make mistakes. I'm certainly that and I've made a lot of mistakes.
Jeffrey Archer

At this point, I can't say what network would be picking it up, but I know that it would be a success.
Christy Romano

I put 150,000 pounds into the stage production of Grease and have got back 1.5 million pounds so far. It has been a fantastic success.
Jeffrey Archer

The only yardstick for success our society has is being a champion. No one remembers anything else.
John Madden

Elegance is not a dispensable luxury but a factor that decides between success and failure.
Edsger Dijkstra

I used to think that losing made you more hungry and determined but after my success at the Olympics and the U.S. Open I realise that winning is the biggest motivation.

Andy Murray

I don't like Tommy on Broadway at all. I like the music, I'm pleased with Pete's success but I don't like what they've done to it.
Roger Daltrey

Picture yourself vividly as winning, and that alone will contribute immeasurably to success.
Harry Emerson Fosdick

My overnight success was really 15 years in the making. I'd been writing songs since I was 6 and playing in bands and performing since I was 14.
Lisa Loeb

You should put time into learning your craft. It seems like people want success so quickly, way before they're ready.
Lucinda Williams

In hindsight, I slid into arrogance based upon past success.
Reed Hastings

If you come into success too soon, you'll burn out and be finished before you know it. If you let the maturation process happen naturally, you'll be happier with yourself in the end.
Lucinda Williams

I'm a mum, so my wardrobe consists of sweaters and jeans. As long as I don't leave the house forgetting my jeans, I count that as a fashion success.
Gail Porter

I'm extremely ambitious. I don't know why people are afraid to say that. I won't sell my soul to the devil, but I do want success and I don't think that's bad.
Jada Pinkett Smith

Former Olympians also get paid to make appearances. Many of them won their medals in an era when Olympic success didn't go hand-in-hand with financial success.
Mary Lou Retton

Success comes to a writer as a rule, so gradually that it is always something of a shock to him to look back and realize the heights to which he has climbed.
P. G. Wodehouse

I just want to continue the success and be an athlete that is shown in a good light in New York City.
Victor Cruz

My wife Elizabeth and I started The Really Terrible Orchestra for people like us who are pretty hopeless musicians who would like to play in an orchestra. It has been a great success. We give performances we've become the most famous bad orchestra in the world.

Alexander McCall Smith

I think people in Botswana are pleased that my books paint a positive picture of their lives and portray the country as being very special. They've made a great success of their country, and the people are fed up with the constant reporting of only the problems and poverty of the continent. They welcome something which puts the positive side.
Alexander McCall Smith

I'm astonished by my success.
Danielle Steel

It's the price of success: people start to think you're omnipotent.
Ben Bernanke

The secret of my success is my hairspray.
Richard Gere

Success, in whatever form it takes, is a tricky thing - once you've achieved your goal, then what? Where do you aim?
Arabella Weir

Your chances of success are directly proportional to the degree of pleasure you desire from what you do. If you are in a job you hate, face the fact squarely and get out.
Michael Korda

It's nice, being brought up with no money at all. It's just not how I measure success, so that makes it a bunch easier.
Bode Miller

Taxation is the price we pay for failing to build a civilized society. The higher the tax level, the greater the failure. A centrally planned totalitarian state represents a complete defeat for the civilized world, while a totally voluntary society represents its ultimate success.
Mark Skousen

Immigrants provide skills that we simply cannot afford to do without. They have contributed hugely to Britain's success.
Charles Kennedy

Independent films have a very different cachet than success films.
Diane Lane

The delusions of self-love cannot be prevented, but intellectual misconceptions as to the means of achieving success may be corrected.
George Henry Lewes

I would love to be a guest on a talk show or a panel that shows women who have been on reality shows

who've had success, to prove to audiences that you don't have to be a fool to become successful.
NeNe Leakes

When making music I sink myself into the process as deeply as I can and forget all of the success.
Enya

I think that everything you do helps you to write if you're a writer. Adversity and success both contribute largely to making you what you are. If you don't experience either one of those, you're being deprived of something.
Shelby Foote

The writing of a melody is an emotional moment success doesn't make it easy.
Enya

Nothing good comes in life or athletics unless a lot of hard work has preceded the effort. Only temporary success is achieved by taking short cuts.
Roger Staubach

It's an awesome responsibility, not only to maintain the level of success the NFL has, but to build on that.
Roger Goodell

Fame and success are very different things.
Enya

It's not just the NFL. Every other league has a draft. It has been fundamental to the success of professional sports.
Roger Goodell

Once you can accept failure, you can have fun and success.
Rickey Henderson

You can take Elvis. You can take Marilyn Monroe. Success and fame will not be the answer if something inside of you is bothering you, if things in your mind aren't going right.
Linda Evans

www.ingramcontent.com/pod-product-compliance
Lightning Source LLC
Chambersburg PA
CBHW070654290526
45790CB00001B/321